CW01496972

URBAN DHARMA

KUSALA BHIKSHU
AND REBECCA WILSON

Printed in the United States of America

First Printing, 2024

ISBN 979-8-9898040-2-3
Black Boat Media

TABLE OF CONTENTS

This book is dedicated to Western Buddhist monks and nuns and the American laypeople who use their practice to make a positive difference in the world.

Foreword

In 2012, I was socially isolated and hovering on the brink of financial disaster. The year before, I'd closed my thriving photography studio in San Diego and moved to Los Angeles, hoping to transition into the film world. Since I'd acquired a few Hollywood connections during a previous career in rock and roll, this hadn't seemed like such a stupid idea at the time. But after a year of interviews, meetings, and "maybes," the best I'd been able to do was land a part-time job off of craigslist, working as a personal assistant for a fitness celebrity. Most of the time, I sat alone in my tiny Hancock Park apartment, barely scraping by as I waited for something to give.

The only part of my life in L.A. that didn't seem to require money or connections was my Buddhist practice. I'd first encountered Buddhism five years earlier, when my friend Kathe dragged me to a weekly meditation group because I wouldn't shut up about my anxiety. The Zen teacher was a tall man named Ken Small, and the group met in the back of a hippie gift shop. I remember we sat on the floor. I think there may have been a Buddha statue. All I know for sure is that the carpet itched. Still, the people seemed bright—"switched on"—and I liked that there was no fee, no evangelizing, and no pressure to speak. Not long after that, I met the Dalai Lama by happenstance, and what had begun as a casual drop-in practice evolved into serious study of Vajrayana Buddhism with a Tibetan monk.

As soon as I arrived in Los Angeles, I set out to find a new Buddhist sangha. I wanted a traditional teacher, preferably Asian, but every Google search sent me to an American monk named Kusala Bhikshu. I resisted at first—I didn't want any watered-down, white-guy Buddhist teachings. Only after I'd tried almost every other group in L.A. did I give the International Buddhist Meditation Center (IBMC) a whirl. Kusala had been ordained since 1994, and I figured that counted for something.

When I arrived at IBMC for my first meditation, it was raining ropes. The place was empty, and stayed that way. Nobody else showed up to the session. So, alongside wind banging against the loose glass of the Zendo, Kusala rang the bell, and he and I sat together. I was distracted by the street noise, low-flying helicopters, and Kusala's cat/sidekick, the appropriately named Rain, who pushed against me as I tried to concentrate. Every single one of those things annoyed me at the time. I later found value in all of them. After the meditation, Kusala offered me a book on bamboo breathing, which I politely declined. He waved goodbye, and on the way to my car, I noticed a few other monks around, all wearing different-colored robes. The monastic diversity was unusual and impressed me enough that I was willing to return. Despite my lukewarm first impression, I began attending meditation at IBMC regularly, and it soon became the one bright spot in my otherwise crash-and-burn Los Angeles life.

I'd been meditating at IBMC for about a year when Kusala overheard me talking about my screenwriting group, and he asked if I could give him feedback on an article he was writing for Koi Pond International. Astonishingly, he made the ho-hum topic of koi fish a good read, and I immediately connected with his humor and voice. I spun up a few edits, and the seed of our writing collaboration was planted.

Soon after, I decided to enroll in Stanford University's Compassion Cultivation Training course. The only problem was that I couldn't afford the housing costs for the program. So, I got creative and found a homeless shelter close to campus that offered room and board in exchange for volunteering in their resource services dayroom. Dorothy's Place had served the people of Salinas, California, for decades. Situated right on Skid Row, it offered snacks, public advocacy, showers, and terrible daytime TV to those living on the street. Anyone applying to be a Dorothy's Place volunteer was required to complete a five-day trial working in the dayroom. Although my bedroom was private and secure, the bathroom, kitchen, and other spaces were shared with people transitioning out of homelessness. Over the course of my trial stay, I saw violence, camaraderie, sickness, compassion, and tremendous suffering. This was my box seat to the human condition—and to how ill-equipped I was to deal with it. My time at Dorothy's Place was a wake-up call, and it changed my view of mental illness and homelessness forever. After the trial period, I waited to hear back from Stanford about my scholarship request. When it was denied, I was a bit relieved. I wasn't sure I was ready to live at Dorothy's Place for another eight weeks. But the experience there had already started to shift my priorities. I decided that instead of spending time in a classroom, studying for a certificate, I could learn a lot more by writing a book about Kusala's community service.

I broached the idea with Kusala, and he agreed to work with me on the project. "It can be a Buddhist *doing* book, not a Buddhist teaching book," he said, which pretty much nailed it. Over the course of the next few months, we met weekly on the porch of IBMC's Quan Yin House. I would drink coffee and ask questions, and we captured the conversations via audio recorder. Not only were the stories better than I'd hoped, but I sensed this could be different than other books authored by monastics. Kusala wasn't talking about Buddhism while sitting in the woods, or on a retreat center cushion. He was offering real-time Buddhist reflections while wading knee-deep in the suffering of city life.

Speaking of the woods—as we neared the end of the recording process, my brother called to ask if I'd be interested in caretaking his house in Maine. It was a welcome shift given my professional struggles in L.A. So I sublet my apartment, bought a one-way plane ticket east, and landed deep in the wilderness with winter fast approaching. Maine proved to be the perfect place to write the book. For the first month, I listened to the recordings on repeat as I raked leaves, stacked wood, and did other country-living chores. From December to May, I awoke at sunrise, lit the wood-burning stove, made coffee, and then wrote for two hours. The first draft of the book was completed in May of 2014. That summer, Kusala and I did the first edit together, reading the manuscript aloud to one another over Skype. I concentrated on structure, place, and story, while Kusala was responsible for the Buddhist wisdom.

In the fall of 2015, I returned to California and rented a room at IBMC for two months while I worked on a video project. I slept on a gym mat and lived out of a suitcase. I didn't realize the value of the experience then, but as soon as I returned to Maine and opened the book files, I found a new strand of the story pouring out of me: the details of Kusala's homelife at the meditation center. These additions necessitated a third rewrite, which we finished in the winter of 2016.

We thought the book was almost ready—but then, life took an unexpected turn. I was hired by Dr. Robert Thurman to become the director of media at the Cultural Center for His Holiness the Dalai Lama in New York City. I left Maine and moved to Manhattan, digitizing the center's historical media into an archive of the Dalai Lama's teachings. Somehow, years passed. During this time, Kusala and I rarely spoke. When my contract ended, I was once again rudderless and jobless—but this time, on the other side of the country. With time on my hands, I called Kusala, and we restarted the book. We were halfway through an editing pass when I was hired as a producer for TED. Again, the book was set aside. We resumed editing in 2021, but my work schedule made our collaboration sporadic. I worried that all the stopping and starting had ruined the project, that the story was disjointed, and that it was all going to hell. In late 2022, we recommitted to a final edit, and Kusala and I met daily over Zoom for read-throughs. At night, I did rewrites. In 2023, nine years after starting the book, we moved toward publishing. Kusala often says, "The right time for something to happen is when it happens." Maybe now I understand.

It is important to say that nobody was paid to write this book, and the publishing costs were completely funded through supporters and crowd-sourced donations. I am deeply thankful to all who gave. The book would not exist without you.

I sincerely hope these stories and reflections shape your perspective on kindness and compassion—for yourself, for others, and for this unpredictable world.

Rebecca Wilson, February 2024

Prologue

In 2001, I set off on a motorcycle journey from Los Angeles to Wisconsin to visit family. This excerpt is from my motorcycle road diary:

The discomfort I felt on the road was my first real sign of freedom. The morning of the first day was tough. It took two hundred miles for the feelings of loss and fear to subside. As I rode out of Los Angeles toward the American backcountry in search of the nameless place, I knew it would be more work than I thought, more work to arrive at the place of "the traveler," where home is wherever there is a shower, and any bed becomes your bed. Where the basics of life find a new dialect, and food, clothing, shelter, and medicine become requisites and royalty.

Was I naive to have embarked on a five-thousand mile motorcycle ride across the U.S. alone? Maybe. But the two-lane roads and hours of aloneness pulled me further into a place I knew nothing about but wanted.

Every day of the ride was different, but the beginning and end turned out to be almost the same. I would awake in the dark, shower, drink water, and go out to the bike, where I'd check the oil and tires and do a visual scan. Then I'd load on the saddlebags, tail pack, and duffle and bungee-net all of it to the back seat. I learned to take the first few miles of every morning slowly to check the bike's balance.

Early on, I knew it was important not to linger in the place where I had slept, be it the KOA or a motel. I could feel my mind attaching to those places, telling me to stay, go back to bed, wait for the waffles to be put out. So I never had coffee or food until I had put in at least a hundred miles. And watching the sunrise on an empty stomach does something to you. The beauty of dawn, even in bad weather, lies in its quietness.

There were obstacles, like construction on bridges, frost heaves in the road, twenty-four-inch potholes, pavement that ended suddenly. I'd stop about every hundred miles to drink something, go to the bathroom, and stretch. Sometimes I would take aspirin before going to sleep. Sometimes when I awoke, the fatigue was painful.

But the hardest obstacles were the inner ones, the doubt about my decision to ride, the feelings around the family awaiting my arrival, thoughts about my future as a monk. Death.

As the landscape roared by, I'd think of the cowboys and wonder how they felt riding solo through this beautiful countryside. The moments of perfection were sharp in contrast to the heat, cold, wind, and rain. These moments would arrive every now and again at strange times, for no apparent reason. "It just can't get any better than this," I thought. And yet it would. The colors, smells, and unity I felt with the road rendered me unthinking to a place within where words have no meaning, no sound, no function. Where time forgets itself, and open space becomes the experience of all things. A place where innate connection soars, and the absence of fear is pure, and you are no longer separate.

Alone but not lonely, connected but not tied, and free from how things used to be. The freedom of the open road called, and my answer each morning was to turn the key and shift into gear.

Chapter 1

Dead & Live Bodies:
The Police Chaplin Years 2000-2007

I rolled to the edge of my futon and sat up, waiting for the tiredness to roll off. I'd been given this room in 1994 after my monastic ordination, and every morning at the meditation center was just a little different, if I stopped to notice. Today, the golden light of Los Angeles poured through the window, filling every corner of the room and reminding me of my aspiration to grow toward an ideal kindness, one that's like sun, falling on everyone equally. Then I was jerked out of sleepiness by a leaf blower that sputtered to a scream just below my window—time to get going. I was due at the morgue anyway.

The International Buddhist Meditation Center (IBMC) isn't what you'd call serene; it's a far cry from the stereotype of a meditation center. For starters, it's wedged in Korea Town, the densest area of Los Angeles.

"K-Town," as it's referred to by most Angelinos, is an island kingdom of sorts where English is a second language and people, cars, and strangeness push down its streets like old blood through small veins. If you love world-class noodle soup, Korean BBQ, and utterly painful massage, it's the place for you. If you're inspired by black spots on the sidewalks, packed buses, and street-side pushcarts selling everything from tacos to USB cables, there's an overcrowded apartment house waiting with your name on it. Being there feels like you've left whatever America is and been dropped halfway around the world in what could be the streets of Seoul in the summertime. And after living there for almost three decades, I understand more about the value of less every day.

"Urban dharma" is a phrase I've coined to describe practicing Buddhism in K-Town, because around every city corner awaits an in-your-face conversation with your suffering, plus everyone else's too.

Although I look like a lost, tall, white tourist walking the streets, I've managed to find a place there, and my admiration for its tightly knit cultural camaraderie has never waned. Somehow, in this time of never-ending phone upgrades and revolving on-demand entertainment, K-Town residents have managed to safe-keep their deeply respected Korean traditions.

In the late afternoon, boba shops fill with tidal movements of formally dating teenagers dressed to the nines like people did in the 1950s. Korean youth regularly give up seats for the elderly; families act with civility; and men and women seem to stay married through thick and thin, for better or worse, only they know.

About ten years after becoming a monk, I planned to escape the city, move to an isolated lake cottage, and buy a sort of "Walden's Pond" place to spend my days meditating among the wild animals and pastoral landscapes. But my teacher had much to say about the idea.

"Here beings are suffering; here is where you can help people," he said. "Who can you serve if you sit on a lake alone?"

Actually, in my mind, it was just a pond. I didn't need a whole lake.

It was then that I truly digested the priorities of a Buddhist practitioner. My teacher didn't say, "Who can you show the way to?" or "Who can you convert?" He simply said, "Who can you serve?" Any sort of service to those in need is the utmost act of a Mahayana Buddhist, so for the next twenty years, I got busy working for free in some pretty hard-to-stomach places.

The Buddha taught two things: that there is suffering, and that there is a way out of it. And you're the only one who can do it for yourself. And an excellent way to start on the Buddhist path is to practice doing acts that lower the world's suffering rather than escalating it. The irony, of course, is that helping others usually reduces your own suffering as well. When it comes to the things you can't change, patience and acceptance lead to balance. It's all about finding the middle path, and trying to stay on it.

The International Buddhist Meditation Center was founded in 1970. It offers a place for those interested in learning about the dharma, which refers to the Buddha's teachings.

Our founder, a respected Vietnamese Buddhist scholar named Venerable Thich Thien-An, was realistic and insightful for the times. He intuited that Americans wouldn't exactly line up to donate cash to an East-Asian Buddhist place, but they likely would pay rent. So for over six decades, IBMC has acted not only as a monastery for Buddhist monks and nuns but has also served the wider public by offering low-income, affordable rental housing. It was a radical move. Monks and nuns on the same grounds, plus forced interaction with secular people—it's still controversial in most circles. But the rental income has provided financial stability and kept our doors open during hard times. We've got no marketing campaign, no community outreach, and nobody's getting rich here, at least in terms of money.

Over the years, I've seen scads of people come and go from IBMC, and many things change, but whatever is the opposite of slick, commercial, and business savvy, that's what we've always managed to be.

People find their way to the center oddly and for different reasons. Some need refuge from their own mind, while others come a bit beaten down by the tiresome modalities of life. Many are financially challenged and have credit issues. Most monastics find that IBMC gives time and space to study, but more importantly, it provides plenty of chances to engage in the teachings. Whether it's practice, affordable housing, or both, you can always find someone willing to share their experience. Some days that's helpful, while other days, not so much.

The IBMC is different from when it first started, but

it still holds diversity as a core value. English-speaking Americans often encounter a high fence of cultural barriers when trying to learn the dharma at an entirely Asian temple. Our founder emphasized teaching Buddhism to English-speaking Americans so Westerners could learn more easily from their peers. This emphasis was a major factor in American Buddhism's first roots in the West.

I made my way downstairs for breakfast tea and thought about the previous weeks of training I'd undergone at the Garden Grove Police Department. Our group of chaplains was on track to start working the ride-alongs shortly. I'd never planned on being part of a police force or wearing a uniform, but life is full of left turns when you're looking right.

The whole thing started when Mayor Broadwater of Garden Grove saw an article about me in the *Los Angeles Times*. He asked someone from his office to approach me about speaking at the mayor's prayer breakfast.

"I don't pray very well," I said, "but I do eat breakfast. Is that good enough?"

And with that, I became the keynote speaker for the city's event.

Years later, this would lead to an invitation to speak at His Holiness the Dalai Lama's eightieth birthday appearance in Garden Grove, an unexpected honor, to say the least. After the mayor's prayer breakfast, a man named Steve LaFond contacted me about joining Garden Grove's volunteer police chaplain program. I said yes, and after a month of background checks and interviews, I started my training. The recruits were from different religious traditions and mirrored Garden Grove's diverse community. Our training included learning police radio protocols; learning how to use the police lights, sirens, and the emergency button to call for help; and learning how to stay out of the way and not get hurt.

We also met with various agencies that work in tandem with the department, such as Social Services, Child Protection, and Probations. Truthfully, the training was dry but important. I sipped the tea and looked at the clock; it was 6:28 a.m., and I had to be at the Orange County Coroner's Office by nine for a dead body field trip, where the chaplains would get exposure to some of the gruesome realities of the job.

Ironically, most of the police chaplain work ended up servicing the living or consoling those who had just lost loved ones. If the deceased person on scene was Buddhist, I would do a few chants if the surviving loved one wished. The chaplains acted as a shoulder to cry on during this confusing time for people. We were just there, providing a friendly interface between the police and civilians. As my Buddhist vows express, I'm to serve all suffering people with kindness, not just the Buddhist ones. I looked more like a cop than a monk in my chaplain's uniform, so nobody saw a Buddhist anyway.

Of course, the Garden Grove coroner's office had a ton of parking, and it's probably the only place in L.A. County that does. There was an undeniable feeling of death hanging outside but no suffering alongside it. It reminded me that only the living churn about in suffering so professionally.

Inside, I expected a waiting room. I imagined a few death industry magazines strewn about, maybe some articles trying to sell the advantages of embalming over cremation. But it turns out that the likelihood of finding a lobby in a coroner's office is low, because they usually aren't open to the public. The morgue is all about the science of life and death, and it's the mortuary that handles all the emotions around it. Loved ones would never want to see what we saw that day. It would be too disturbing: the bodies cut open, hanging akwardly in unnatural states. Being closed to the public was a good idea.

As I walked down the hallway toward an empty desk, the only sign of life was an abandoned cup of steaming ramen soup. I looked around, but there was nobody. The room had that certain governmental feel, formal and taut.

I walked down a small hall toward two wooden doors.

"Just sign in," a voice said.

I turned back to see the deputy coroner stirring the noodles.

"The Catholic and Baptist are already here," he said. "We're just waiting on a few more."

"Thanks," I said, picking up the clipboard.

There were ten police chaplains in our training class: a Muslim, a rabbi, a priest, about six Christians, and me, the Buddhist guy. The group struck me as odd, and the only things we had in common were sensible shoes and mostly good posture. Other than that, our ideas on death, dying, and life were wildly divergent.

So there we stood, religious people, congregated around

the sign-in desk, watching the deputy coroner's noodle soup go down in silence. It was a welcome icebreaker when Steve LaFond, from the community relations office, appeared with his usual enthusiasm.

"Hi, everyone. Hope the traffic wasn't too bad."

We all shook our heads the way only L.A. people can when it comes to traffic.

Steve led our group through the big wooden doors and down a short hallway into an empty, vault-like room. It felt barren in an unusual way, vacant and uncomfortable. The carpet was that sort of utilitarian, short pile, "city and county" carpet, and it didn't smell like anything, not even air. The only thing in the room was one large, long, navy blue curtain that hung halfway down a wall. It was covering something, and the whole affair was just plain eerie.

"Well," Steve said, looking at a clipboard, "six bodies came in last night." He sounded like an inventory manager at The Gap.

The deputy coroner pulled the navy drape to the side, revealing a large, thick glass window. We peered through it as if looking into a giant fish tank. But instead of glinting tropical fish, we saw pale, naked bodies lying on stainless steel tables. Three of them had washcloth-sized towels covering their faces. It was surreal. The Muslim in our group stepped back from the window just as I stepped forward, and we clumsily bumped, like some poorly staged sitcom. I was used to being awkward—I'm six foot two—but he seemed a little flustered.

The closest body was right below the window. Two

people wearing hazmat suits stood over an Asian woman and pointed into her chest cavity. She lay cut open from the stomach to the neck, and her breasts hung awkwardly to either side, like half-filled water balloons slung over a clothesline. One of the doctors was spinning a large-handled crank that reminded me of a woodworking clamp. We watched as he slowly cranked her rib cage open, twisting the clamp's handle like a can opener. The other doctor carefully reached inside and felt around. It reminded me of the kids' board game Operation, which made a zapping noise if you touched the body as you reached inside.

Most of the lab instruments were surprisingly basic and had the feel of the 1950s. A small ball-nosed hammer, large loop-handled scissors, basic saws, and clamps lay neatly on caster-legged tables. I found it fitting that examining death, one of the oldest natural processes, required only the most basic instruments.

A tech grabbed some long-handled scissors that looked like hedge trimmers my father owned in the '70s, only she didn't have a cigarette hanging from her mouth. She pushed the handles together and cut deep into the rib cage, the bone springing open like a tree branch freed from a tangle of kite string.

On the far side of the examining room, two males huddled over some paperwork. The whole thing felt like peering through a hole in a shoe box; inside was a well-lit, dead-body diorama.

"On scene," Steve said, "the smell can get pretty bad, depending on a bunch of stuff. Some officers smoke cigars to counter the smell, but bring essential oils if you'd like."

The word *essential* had finally earned its place on those tiny brown bottles.

"Do not bring VapoRub," he continued, turning more serious. "All it does is open your passages, so you and everyone around you will smell everything more."

I looked back at the Asian woman's body. She was in her early thirties and had long, thick hair. With her midsection hanging open, every organ and sinew of tissue stared up at us.

"She died of an overdose," Steve said. "The neighbor's dog found her on the side of their house in the grass. They think she stumbled away from a party, walked across the street, and passed out. She choked on her vomit."

I thought of Jimi Hendrix.

A thick silence had filled the room as the group stood motionless, face-to-face with our inevitable. In our line of work, talking about death came easily, but staring it down and standing in the wordless areas around it didn't.

What was evident was that the woman lying before us hadn't planned to die that night. Her hair was a bit tousled yet held the styled hairdo from the night before. Her brows were well-groomed arches. A bit of lipstick still sat at the corners of her mouth. What looked most out of place were her freshly painted, pearl-white fingernails. They shined electric next to her dark skin. And her organs were sculptural, the twists and turns perfectly housed like peas in a pod, everything shaped in tandem with whatever neighbored it, all things interconnected, all things interdependent. The whole thing looked like a Salvador Dali painting.

"What's that bright yellow stuff?" I asked, pointing at a yellow string that weaved through her abdomen.

"That's fat," Steve said.

"Kinda makes ya think twice the next time you want fast food," said the priest.

I was the only one who laughed.

"She came in about 4 a.m. They're putting T.O.D. about two," said the deputy.

"So would we be called to a scene like this?" asked the Muslim.

"Absolutely. You're on whatever scene the officer you're riding with gets called to. It could be a cat in a tree or something like this. Your job's to serve in whatever capacity helps the officer or the community." Steve turned and squared up to us. "It's not only about what you do. It's also about what you represent."

We all stared blankly. The Christian woman asked, "What do we represent?"

"Kindness. You represent the voice of kindness in situations that need it. You're the compassionate activity of the police department," Steve said. "Often, the officers are so busy at the scene that they have very little time to interact with the family and friends of the victim. That's where you come in."

I liked that. Our purpose made sense now.

We looked back into the exam room. The two female technicians continued pushing various bodies over to the window, each with its own story. One man was discovered dead in his La-Z-Boy chair, clutching the neck of a vodka bottle. His hand was frozen in rigor mortis as if his bottle was still there. Next to his body lay his liver on a tray; it was the size of a small brown throw pillow.

There was also a fourteen-year-old boy who came in as a suicide. He'd hung himself because he didn't get the grades he wanted. His younger sister found him dangling from an extension cord in the garage.

"If you're called to a messy scene, like a shooting, most of the time there'll be hazmat cleaning services there, taking care of fluids," Steve said.

"What a job to have," the priest mumbled.

"When there's a lot of blood," the deputy said, "it can coagulate into this Jell-O-like consistency in only a few hours; sometimes they just shovel it into bags, but brain matter, that's hard. Once it dries, it's like cement. If the putty knives can't scrape it off, they bring in a steam injection machine to melt it off."

Fitting, I thought. Even when we're dead, the mind still clings to stuff.

I took another once-over at the bodies; they looked like parade balloons that had lost half their helium. I tried to imagine my body lying there, someone looking at me through the glass, but I didn't want to go there. I'd save that for later on the meditation cushion.

In some Buddhist schools, there's a practice called the "cemetery meditation," in which you contemplate the decomposition of a body. *The Tibetan Book of the Dead* details how to practice dying using sleep cycles. It's a way to prepare for the moment of passing. The practice is supposed to help develop a familiarity with the dying process and what's experienced before what the Buddhists call the *bardo*. It's believed to be a tunnel or state of being between this life and the next. It's not just for Buddhists, though; it's believed to be part of the rebirth process for all living things.

Nirvana is freedom from going through that tunnel again, bypassing rebirth into the next cycle of existence. It's not that we never die again; we're never reborn to die again. Well, it's the same thing in some circles, I guess.

One of the doctors rolled the table with the suicide boy right under our window. The room's gravity doubled. It's disturbing to see a dead child. The Muslim was standing quietly, frozen. One of the priests stood shifting uneasily from side to side. The poker-faced rabbi looked away and fidgeted with a pen in his shirt pocket. The self-inflicted death of a fourteen-year-old was a special kind of disturbing. Maybe the deepest type of suffering.

The coroner broke the silence. "We've got a storage cooler on the side of the building where the deceased are kept. We just spent a pretty good chunk of change upgrading the security out there. We've caught a few kids trying to break in for a look."

Humans have such a fascination with death, yet we're so ill-equipped to contemplate our own.

One of the techs picked up a scalpel and set to work on the alcoholic's head. She skillfully sliced him from ear to ear and peeled the skin forward, letting the excess drape over his face like a plastic Halloween mask.

"It's bad enough he's dead, but now he can't even see," the Baptist joked.

Nobody laughed; this was all too real.

The doctor spooled up a drill that I swear I'd seen in Home Depot the week before. She made a small, precise hole through the skull like a pro, then took some brain matter and checked it under a microscope.

"Once we had a serial killer's body, and there was"— Steve paused, searching for words—"heaviness isn't the right word…" he stammered, "evil isn't the right word, but it's not the wrong one either. It's hard to describe. It was fear, I guess. I felt fear being around that body."

Later, Steve revealed that he was a Mormon, and that working at the morgue helped him reconnect with his faith.

Our field trip to the coroner's office concluded with a presentation not unlike the kind you get in driver's ed. They sat us in a small classroom for the screening of a bizarre film that could have been called *Gruesome On-Scene Deaths by David Lynch*.

One man was hit by a train; his head was torn off. Another died while removing a tree from his yard; it had fallen in the wrong direction and landed on him, crushing him into the hole he'd dug. We also were shown a victim of kinky, erotic asphyxiation. The man was found hanging dead, wearing women's makeup and a bra with his pants down around his ankles.

After the film, I felt a little overwhelmed. Queasy. Ready to leave. Steve gave us the contact information for getting our bulletproof vests. As we all gathered our things, one of the Christian chaplains pulled a box of lemon muffins from his bag. "I brought a snack if anyone wants some?"

What a way to end the dead body field trip. Muffins. It harkened back to grade school as everyone chewed and sipped water from their little paper water cooler cups. The surrealism swept through me, the words of conversations dropped into only sound, and I could somehow see our group in a strange, interconnected moment. We humans appeared like animals now; our shared genus and behaviors had so much in common. There was a visible undercurrent of shared anima. Starting at death had somehow abstracted our human ways; our bodies, sounds, and gestures seemed foreign yet also recognizable. This was possibly how cats might see us.

"There's one left, Kusala. You want this?" someone asked, jarring me. I looked down at the Catholic's outstretched arm, the Ziploc bag with a small muffin dangling from its end.

"Ah, no, but thank you," I said.

"Sure?"

"I never take the last of anything," I said, gathering my things. "But thanks."

As I stepped out into the afternoon, the urgency of life now simmered in the air between the trees. I could die. Now. Today. That lemon muffin could have been my last bite of food. We worry so much about tomorrow with the confidence that tomorrow will come.

At the stoplight, my motorcycle idled with a perfect hum. As irony would have it, the morgue was right across from South Coast Plaza Mall, one of the largest, most exclusive shopping experiences in Southern California. The parking lot was packed. A BMW trolled for a spot, and a woman on foot zigzagged between cars in her perfected stiletto gait. The mall valets sprinted about, and I imagined their internal organs jostling as they jogged, bouncing inside their bellies like snuggly packed luggage.

We focus most of our lives on accruing wealth and push ourselves to the brink of insanity with worry over losing it. No wonder people come to me asking how to get rid of their anxiety.

Accepting life's groundlessness and impermanence is a throughline in Buddhist teachings. Clinging to circumstance, belongings, relationships, and our identity is futile, like trying to stop the stars from shining. We repeatedly suffer over it. When we die, what matters? Not our jobs, our belongings, or even our families. Death is a solo affair, no carry-on baggage allowed. We're muscled into saying goodbye to what we relentlessly lived to acquire. We repeatedly hear this cliché, but we all still literally buy into it.

As I pulled onto the 405 freeway, I felt alive and focused on staying that way. It was a scorching L.A. summer day, but I didn't mind.

The heat brought back memories of the times before ordination. It was 1994 and I was driving down Ocean Boulevard in Santa Monica, listening to Don Henley. In just a few months, I'd become a novice monk and start my new job as IBMC's residential manager. So if I were going to live it up, now was the time. But all I wanted to do was go to the beach. I'd already done all the "live it up" stuff. That's what got me there. None of it seemed to bring me any feelings of contentment.

Lots of people are unclear about the monastic ordination process. Some people seem to think it's just a piece of paper, while others have asked if I was put in front of a court of bald monks and asked rapid-fire questions about Buddhist scripture. Most assume there's a written test. It's not like the DMV or anything, I usually say. But the reality is, it varies greatly among Buddhist sects. It's partly a legal ceremony, partly a personal affair, partly a cultural tradition, and an entirely humbling, exciting, and meaningful act of dedication. Among the various Buddhist schools, there is one common denominator: a vow of commitment to the teachings.

Before ordination, I'd been working a full-time job and living alone in a small apartment in Palms, on the west side of Los Angeles. In preparation for the change, I sold most of my belongings, gave away the rest, trashed my bed, and bought a new futon. I ended up selling my guitar, banjo, and keyboard, thinking I wouldn't be playing those again. (Funny how things unravel down the road.)

It was a unique chance to purge things that caused attachment. My "Icons of Motown" drink coaster set was hard to let go of. Looking back, I laugh at my delusions. I believed that giving up these things would free me, but I quickly learned that attachment is rooted in the mind, not the stuff. It's a lifelong practice of catch and release.

After ordination, in my new job at IBMC as the residential manager, I'd be vetting potential renters before the Residential Action Committee (RAC) interviewed them. They'd get the final thumbs up or down on the prospective tenant. I'd finish the process by signing the lease and going over conduct guidelines. After all, it was a meditation center, so we didn't want certain things going on. Most of the rules were straightforward, created to support the community, but it wasn't rare that a new resident would go south, forgoing payment or doing something crazy. My job was to get them back on track, try and keep harmony in the houses, and bring a "can't we all just get along" attitude and mindset.

I clearly remember my first morning as an ordained novice monk. I stood in front of the mirror, not totally sure what I saw. I looked different, and it wasn't the missing hair or the new robes. It was something else, something there are no words for. It was a moment I can recall like it was yesterday, but I still have no clarity on what changed. I only knew something had.

Reverend Karuna Dharma gave me an upstairs bedroom in the zendo where I still currently reside after twenty-seven years. She also arranged for full health insurance and a small monthly stipend for me to buy food, socks, gas, etc. Any money that came to me through donations, speaking engagements, weddings, and so on would be mine to keep. At the end of the year, I was given an independent contractor 1099 tax form, and it was up to me to pay any taxes. I felt lucky to have the basics covered. Most people spend their whole life chasing that.

Plus I had no credit card debt, and my motorcycle was paid off. All I needed was motor vehicle insurance, which wasn't much for a bike. And I didn't have to worry about dating or entertainment. My new life would be one of autonomy and simplicity, lean.

After ordination, I was all in, for better or for worse. Nowadays, I'm happy to report it's mostly neither.

The morning after the trip to the coroner's office, I was standing in the kitchen of IBMC making toast when Marcus, one of the residents, came through the back door, frantic and out of breath.

"Shin collapsed," he said. "Deadra is calling an ambulance!"

I followed him outside and down two houses to Ananda Hall, where the nun lived.

I climbed the stairs to her room to find Shin lying on the floor, unmoving. She'd been at the center for about two years, and although I knew her well, I never felt like I did. She'd had medical issues most of her life and had been under the supervision of a few doctors, and now it appeared her new medications weren't mixing well. One of her housemates held her hand, and another stood over her.

Deadra, who rented the room next door, sobbed. "Kusala, it was this huge crash, and when I came in, she was on the ground, shaking."

Shin had landed on her side. I put my hand on her shoulder. I felt helpless.

"Did it seem like a seizure?" I asked.

Deadra nodded. I'd seen someone seize once before, when I was nineteen. I'd taken a "traveling job" on a magazine sales team, which turned out to be a scam. They came to Wisconsin, recruited boys and girls right out of high school, and promised us a big life in the Big Apple. They gave us a Saturday morning training session over pancakes at a local waffle house and then loaded us into a van; the next stop was Brooklyn, where we received $5 a day. We were expected to sell magazines door to door and had to reach an astronomical quota before we could make another cent. It would have been illegal by today's standards.

One of the girls ended up getting pregnant and got sent home, and the other girl had her first epileptic seizure on the bathroom floor of a motel. That's when I first learned of them.

"Hello! Hello!" Carl yelled down the hall. Our special needs tenant was home and just coming up the stairs. "Hello....everyone?"

Carl poked his head into Shin's room and gasped with surprise.

Caroline moved toward him. "She's not dead."

I looked up at Marcus. "Can you pick that up?" I said, glancing at the small Buddha statue that had been knocked to the floor."How long ago did you call the ambulance?" I asked.

Time dragged, but finally the ambulance arrived. Deadra ran to the window. "It's a fire truck!" she yelled. As she raced downstairs, I stayed with Shin, who was barely breathing.

Soon two medics and four firemen surrounded Shin. Within minutes she was being carried down the stairs on a gurney. Outside, every apartment building balcony was lined with people watching. One of the firemen gave us a once-over and asked, "Is this some kinda halfway house?" I squinted and scanned our motley crew. I shook my head no.

I hurried back to Shin's room, grabbed her purse, wrapped the small gold Buddha in a clean washcloth, and dropped it into her purse.

Outside, I brought her purse to the medic. "It'll probably be good if she has this when she wakes up," I said. "I'll call her sister."

He looked at the bag. "I can't take that, sorry, protocol."

The doors of the ambulance slammed shut, thudding like a walk-in fridge. As the truck sped off and the sirens faded, a silence descended over the front lawn. Nobody moved. It was like we were waiting for something. Carl was the first to peel off, and eventually we all trickled away, clicked back into our day. I was due to teach in an hour, so Marcus took Shin's purse to the emergency room at UCLA Medical Center on the west side of town. Shin died four hours later.

Thankfully, her sister made it to the hospital just before she passed, and later, I went to say goodbye. I was shocked standing there, seeing her body starkly inanimate, but I took comfort in seeing that the little gold Buddha statue had made it from her purse to her hospital bedside table.

That night at the center, I looked in her room for a picture and found a small framed photo of Shin in her nun's robes. I added it to the center's memorial altar. It's a place in the zendo where we display pictures of all who've passed in our community. All kinds of people are honored there: kids, the elderly, monks, nuns, police, parents, astronauts; it's quite a sight. It's intended to remind us of impermanence, of the inevitable ending of all life, of our death.

I found a spot for Shin's picture next to my teacher, Dr. Ratanasara, who'd died about three years earlier.

He passed in his room at the center. Cancer. When I went to see his body, I swear he had a smile. I was taken aback by how peaceful and youthful he appeared. A significant aspect of Buddhism involves dying well in order to attain a good rebirth. Dr. Ratanasara was an adept practitioner and looked like he had left in good spirits, which is important for a passing Buddhist. Some schools say your last thought in this life is the first thought in the next, so it's vital that you leave with compassion and kindness in your heart during the transition, avoiding panic, fear, regret, and most of all, anger.

I came under fire in the lay community for taking a picture of Dr. Ratanasara's dead body. After he passed, I sent the image to people who loved him, thinking they'd want it. It's common to do so in many Eastern cultures, and sometimes even expected. But a few people didn't like it. I felt terrible. However, the center selected that picture for our memorial wall, where it still hangs today. His smile and death are memorialized.

Buddhists don't hide death as most people do. Often times the body of the deceased is left undisturbed, sometimes for days, until all the visitors have come and the monastics have completed the death ceremonies.

As I stood looking at Shin's picture on the memorial wall, I thought, *You never know what's about to happen.* I was sure she would share that sentiment. I exhaled, thinking of the time when my picture would be there.

As I retired to my room, I passed the kitchen and saw my morning toast poking up from the toaster untouched. Who'd have thought that two houses down, Shin was taking her last conscious breaths while the bread was browning? I took a bite of the cold toast and then threw it out.

As I lay in the dark that night, waiting to fall asleep, the day's events flashed through my mind. "Is this a halfway house?" rang through my head. Although it hadn't started out that way, some-forty-odd years later, it wasn't far from the mark.

After ordination, I was getting used to the new job at IBMC. I started a weekly dharma talk in the evening. First we meditated, then I did a half-hour talk. We concluded with Q&A. I learned how much I didn't know every week and ended up traveling regularly to the Bodhi Tree Bookstore in search of answers. My personal library quickly grew, and so did my knowledge. They say you don't know something until you try and teach it, and I've found that to be true.

The College of Buddhist Studies was in full swing, and in November 1996, I received my BA. My teacher, Venerable Dr. Ratanasara, was president of the college. Courses were conducted in the Thien-an House on the property. The Abbess Rev. Karuna Dharma and the head monk, Sarika Dharma, kept things running. All of the IBMC staff lived on the property. Dr. Ratanasara, among other things, was the founder of the Buddhist Sangha Council of Southern California and the co-founder of the Los Angeles Buddhist/Catholic Dialogue. I attended weekly classes at the college, joined the Buddhist/Catholic dialogue every month, and continued my urban monk's training at the meditation center.

The student-teacher relationship I had with Dr. Ratanasara was like that of a spiritual father and son. I asked many questions about Buddhism and the lifestyle of a monk in Sri Lanka. He allowed the ancient ways of Buddhism to slowly unfold for me. Talking to him was like stepping into a time machine; I could travel back through stories from centuries before and begin to understand the mindset of monks and how everything they did had a purpose for training their minds. It was up to me to practice these teachings in IBMC's contemporary urban enviorment. I came to understand that my meditation practice was a refuge, as was my room. With all the stuff going on at the center, it was sometimes difficult to feel peace and ease. But that was our founder's intent—good fodder for practice.

Life in Korea Town includes gangs, traffic, graffiti, and deafening truck buzzers that alert pedestrians of impending doom. The helicopters fly so low you can see the face of the pilot, and if he shaved that morning.

I'd guess it's not what the Buddha had imagined. Back then, nobody needed money for transportation to give a dharma talk. The ever-increasing urban population kept giving me suffering people to help. Yep, it was a new ball game, different from the Buddha's time for sure. You can't learn if nothing challenges you.

After the trip to the coroner, our police chaplain homework was to get a bulletproof vest and to meet the following week at the shooting range.

After vows, I'd done my best never to harm a bug. I hadn't counted on holding a gun, let alone being trained by the police to fire one properly.

I wasn't actually sure that I could. Maybe this wasn't for me after all, I thought. When I get these moments of questioning, I'm always reminded of a wise thing my first teacher said. "Roll in it, not over it or around it, but just roll in it." My first teacher was Shinzen Young, and he was very much American. It was 1979, and he said things that sounded like he'd lifted them from a Bob Dylan song. He was an incredibly helpful influence on me for years. I might not be here today if he hadn't been an English-speaking native and a good communicator.

Back at the center, I phoned the facility that issued bulletproof vests and made an appointment for the end of the week.

When I arrived, I was in street clothes, and the woman at the front desk gave me some paperwork. "Know your measurements?"

"XL," I said.

"No, your chest, arms, and waist?"

"Oh, no. I haven't worn a suit in a while."

She smiled. "Just fill in what you can and bring it back up."

Another woman came to get me and took me back to a large locker room filled floor to ceiling with metal cages. In some of the lockers hung riot gear; in others were various protective gloves and boots. There were also head-to-toe suits of body armor. It was astounding how much safety gear was needed for an officer to stay safe on the job.

"Have you ever shot a gun?"

"Yeah," I said, "way back in military high school, when I was a kid."

We went through four models of vests and a few sizes until we found one that fit.

"And Mr. Kusala," she said as I left, "don't go getting shot now, ya hear?"

Those words would ring through me every time I strapped on that vest. She had made it real for me, that the vest wasn't just for show. Until then, I'd digested all the safety talks like the airplane emergency instructions they give you before takeoff. Just a formality. But now her comment hung before me like the oxygen mask you never actually expect to see.

As I walked out to the motorcycle carrying the vest, I thought about the amount of insanity and suffering in the world, how humans had created bullets and now vests to stop them.

A squad car was parked next to my bike, and an officer was getting out.

He moved with agility, but now I could see the vest beneath.

"Are those the new ones?" he said, pointing to the vest in my hand.

"I don't know. It's my first one."

"Oh, you're new? How's it going?"

"Oh, no, actually I'm just a chaplain."

He froze and gave me the once over. "Wow, okay. You're pretty brave," he said, smiling.

I flashed a questioning look.

"We've gotten lots of training," he said, backpedaling. "I mean, you guys, you've hardly been trained at all."

I didn't realize what he meant until the time I was riding with an officer and we stopped a man driving a car with a gun lying on the seat next to him. I had no idea what to do or think. Everything just went quiet.

When you wear a bulletproof vest, it's a physical statement of the violence in the world, but as. As chaplains, we were symbols of peace and kindness. Some days, that was hard to reconcile.

The following week, the chaplains trained at the gun range. We learned how to retrieve and fire the police car shotgun. My high school military target practice came right back, and the chaplains were shocked that the Buddhist, who represented the most thorough set of nonviolent ideals, had the best shot.

After all the training courses, the trip to the morgue, the well-fitted bulletproof vest, six sessions at the target range, and an extensive background check, I was finally cleared to start. A few of the chaplains had fallen by the wayside; some felt the commitment too big, and others didn't know we'd have to handle guns, so our team ended up being only six to eight people. We'd do the volunteer shifts on our own time with no pay. We'd simply call up, book ourselves a week out, and arrive in our black jeans, black shoes, and our black polo shirt with the vest beneath. We were also provided with a black nylon jacket that read CHAPLAIN in big white letters on the back. The purpose of the jacket was to make sure we weren't mistaken for police officers, but it felt like people saw me as a cop anyhow.

The chaplain's program was pretty flexible. You could do as many ride-alongs as you liked, but you had to do at least one every thirty days. The only other requirement was the monthly dinner meeting, where we'd talk about new procedures, share thoughts, and ask questions. Steve LaFond was an excellent group facilitator and had answers for all of our hard questions, like "What do you say to a child who watches their father get cuffed and taken away?"

I learned lots about Garden Grove and couldn't have been more in the right place. Located in Orange County, the town has the second-highest population of Vietnamese-Americans in the United States. And even though the highly publicized Christian Crystal Cathedral broadcasts to thousands from Garden Grove, the town is still is heavily Buddhist.

I arrived for my first shift and was assigned a car and a partner. Now, these guys had no idea they would have me in their car until the day of the ride-along. So on a few occasions, the officers groaned a bit, which is understandable. I was an added liability to their day. Not only did they have to conduct their affairs under the constant threat of unpredictable violence, but now they had a six-foot-two, not-so-agile white guy next to them to worry about.

The first ride-along was a bit strange. The officer said very little to me. We just drove around in silence for the most part. The shift was noon to midnight. It was quiet until a domestic disturbance call came in.

He punched in the address, flipped on the siren, and things went from sleepy to *Dukes of Hazzard* in just a few breaths. Watching the traffic in front of us magically unzip as we barreled along was thrilling. When we got stuck behind a driver who was oblivious, the officer gave a loud staccato "Bleep," and the car moved to the side. I peered into the car's window as we passed.

"Elderly?" the officer asked.

"Very," I said.

"We try never to go lights and sirens when we pass the big retirement home on the north side. It can create lots of panic in there, sometimes health issues."

As we rounded the block near our destination, he shut off the siren and lights and quietly coasted to a stop in front. The two-bedroom home was your average 1970s tan stucco with a gravel yard.

"Should I stay here?" I asked, feeling a sudden nervous heat under my vest. I'd never imagined the moment I'd arrive on a police scene wearing protective armor, with only about forty-three hours of proxy training.

"Kind of defeats the purpose, wouldn't it?" he said.

I fell in behind him as we walked up the sidewalk.

We stood at the door and took a beat, listening. Nothing. Then he reached up and gave a perfect cop door knock. Quick. Measured. And it undeniably meant business. Inside, a woman erupted in Vietnamese. I couldn't understand a word of it, but I didn't need to. Her suffering was obvious.

A tall, lanky man matter-of-factly answered the door. He acted as if we were selling Girl Scout cookies.

"Hello, officers," he said calmly with a smile. He reminded me of my seventh-grade teacher.

"Sir," the officer said, "we've received a—"

The screaming erupted again. It was coming from the back of the house.

"Sir, what's going on?"

The man's posture collapsed as he rubbed at one eye.

"Everything's fine; it's my wife. We're just fighting."

"Fighting's not illegal, sir, but causing a disturbance is."

The husband looked over his shoulder toward the noise.

"We need to check on her welfare, sir."

The man didn't move.

"Any physical altercations tonight?"

"No."

"Well, someone called, and that's why we're here. Can we come in?"

Worry washed through his eyes.

"It's routine that we look around to make sure everyone's all right."

The man yelled down the hallway in Vietnamese to the woman.

Silence returned.

He stared at us, and we stared at him.

The woman started up again, and whatever she was shouting, it was the same thing, repeatedly, except now she had tears in her voice.

The man erupted. "SHUT UP, will you! It's the police!"

She fell silent again. You could practically hear her thoughts, though I couldn't understand them. None of us moved; an invisible thread of pause connected us all.

"Sir, can she come to the door?"

"No, she's drunk." He rubbed his eye again.

"I need her to come to the door. I need to see her, or we'll need to come in, sir." The officer stepped into the doorframe.

The man exhaled, tired and defeated, and stepped aside, letting the front door swing wide.

"You can come in, but she's really drunk."

Two Asian silk paintings hung on one wall of the living room, and an oversized Denver Broncos football flag hung on another. A Jack in the Box commercial played on a muted TV. The big white bubblehead Jack drove the family along in a station wagon.

"Usually she just passes out," the man said, "but she's had a lot of coffee today, and she's on this new medicine for high blood pressure. Maybe it's a side effect."

"Ma'am?" the officer called with a perfect blend of compassion and authority.

"Ma'am? My name is Officer Devon, police. I'm here to check on your welfare. Can you step out here for a second?"

She didn't answer.

"Is she injured?" the officer asked.

"No, just mad."

"You two are married?"

The man nodded.

He rattled something off in Vietnamese that was met with more silence.

"Does she speak English?" the officer asked.

"Depends on the day, but she understands it fine."

"Ma'am, if you don't come out here, I have to come back there," said Officer Devon.

The man's hands twisted inside his pleated pant pockets.

Officer Devon stepped toward the hallway. "Ma'am, I'm coming back there. I just need to confirm your safety, okay?" He looked back at us. "What is she yelling?"

The man looked away, his face souring. "I don't know."

I stood taking in the whole of the situation. I was worried about what we'd find at the end of the hallway.

"She threw an alarm clock at me, and it broke a huge mirror on the door," the man said. "That's probably why someone called you," he confessed. "Nobody was hurt, though; it was just loud."

Officer Devon stood in the hallway, looking at the closed door. A slit of light lined the bottom.

"Sir, can you get her to come out here?"

"She won't listen when she's this drunk."

"Okay, can you please just have a seat on the couch for us then?"

The man did, and Officer Devon continued to walk toward the door.

"My name is Officer Devon, police. I can't leave here till we do a welfare check on you, ma'am. We just need to say hello."

The silence welled louder.

In the silence that followed, we stood outside the bedroom door. Officer Devon leaned in for a listen, then tapped gently. "Ma'am, can you come out here for a minute?"

The husband appeared at the end of the hallway, and Officer Devon barked, "Sir, please stay on the couch!"

The man quickly disappeared back to the living room. I had to admire the vocal dexterity of the police. They can say, "Sit down, sir" ten different ways, depending on what's going on.

Officer Devon grabbed the doorknob. "Ma'am? I'm a police officer, I'm coming in, and I just need to confirm that you're not hurt."

The silence bled from under the door.

"We're coming in now," Devon said, resting his hand on his gun. Then he turned the knob and pushed open the door.

We both stood looking.

Large shards of jagged glass stuck up like butterfly wings from the shag carpet. Tangled in the mess was a 1980s snooze bar alarm clock, the kind with red blinking dots.

The woman was in her sixties and was sitting on her bed. She stared vacantly in our direction but didn't seem to grasp that we were there.

"Ma'am, my name is Officer Devon. I'm a police officer." He said this as if she were a hurt bird in a corner.

She had the slight sway of drunkenness.

"Ma'am, are you all right?" Devon asked.

Her eyes were swollen, her cheeks were wet, but she wasn't crying now.

"Ma'am?"

"No," she said.

"Are you hurt?"

"Yes," She said.

Officer Devon stepped onto the glass; it crunched like Grape-Nuts under his boot.

"Where are you hurt, ma'am?".

She pointed to her chest. "Sad," she said.

At that moment, I noticed a small shrine set up on a table next to the closet. Lit with an electric candle, various trinkets surrounded a picture of a youthful Vietnamese man.

She looked at me and pointed to the glass on the floor.

"Shoes, the shoes," she said.

I went to the front door, where I'd seen the shoes, and returned with a black pair of slippers.

"Looks like your toe is bleeding," Officer Devon said.

I handed her the slippers, and her eyes awakened from their drunken haze, registering the kindness of a stranger.

"Thank you," she said.

"Let's go out to the living room and take a look at your toe," said Officer Devon.

She nodded without an ounce of fight and took hold of our arms, using them like steady rods as we all made our way through the glass.

In the living room, she sat at the farthest end of the couch, away from her husband. She refused even to acknowledge him.

"You're very drunk," Officer Devon said.

She nodded in agreement.

"You drink a lot?" he asked.

"She drinks all the time since her son died," her husband said.

She hissed a spur of Vietnamese at him.

"It's only been six months," he continued. "He borrowed my car that day."

The silence returned.

Officer Devon took a deep breath. "I'm so sorry for your loss, both of you. I think the grief of losing a child is the worst grief there is."

She looked up at him.

"A lot of people drink during periods like this," he said, "but if you throw things, cause disturbances, the neighbors will call the police and we have to come."

She nodded.

"This is the first time," her husband said.

"We're never here on the first time," Officer Devon said.

The man's eyes dropped.

"Have you looked into getting her help for the drinking?" Officer Devon said.

"She won't do it. Everything I suggest she just hates."

"Well." Officer Devon turned to her. "I'm suggesting it, not him. I think you need to get some help for your drinking, do you understand?"

She nodded. Officer Devon moved toward the door. "I've got some information in the car. Be right back."

With that, he left me standing in the room, the two of them sitting on the couch, looking up at me like kids in the principal's office.

She said something to her husband in Vietnamese.

He looked at me. "She's asking if you're a policeman?"

"No." I shook my head.

She said more; he translated. "What do you do then?"

"I'm a helper," I said.

She stared at me, wanting more.

"I'm a Buddhist chaplain," I said, pointing to the CHAPLAIN letters on my hat.

"Buddhist?" she said.

I nodded. A *but you're not Asian* look shot across her face.

That morning I'd slipped a small picture of Quan Yin into my shirt pocket as an extra shim of protection. It was given to me by my teacher many years back. Quan Yin is the female bodhisattva of compassion and mercy; her full name, Guanshiyin, means "Observing the sounds (or cries) of the world."

I pulled the picture out and handed it to her. With sudden recognition, she stared at it and said, "Quan Yin!"

She looked back up at me with warmth.

"My teacher gave me that many years ago," I said.

She smiled, clasped it between her palms, and gave me a little bow. She held it against her heart and slipped it into the front of her bra.

"My teacher gave me that," I reiterated. "I've had that a long time," I said pleadingly.

She leaned forward, grabbing my hand.

"Thank you," she said, her eyes filling with tears.

I bent and handed her a box of Kleenex from the side table and said a silent goodbye to my special Quan Yin.

Officer Devon came back inside with some pamphlets. "Here are some support resources," he said. "I've seen lots of people create a second crisis after a first by trying to drink things away. Maybe both of you can use a little help with all of it?"

"I doubt if she'll go," the husband said, but his wife snatched the papers as if to spite him.

We said our goodbyes and made our way to the car. We stayed parked outside the house for a while as Officer Devon wrote out some notes for the report. I thought about the parents' dead son and what it must be like to lose a child. I thought of Quan Yin and knew that picture could do way more for that mother than it ever could for me.

Officer Devon started the car, and I looked back toward the house. Through the small front window, I could see that the husband had moved to the ottoman and sat facing his wife like a shoe salesperson. He was hunched over her foot, carefully dabbing it with Kleenex.

We drove a few blocks. "Good job back there," Officer Devon said.

"I didn't really do anything."

"That's why it was good. Most people try to do something when nothing is usually all that's required for a situation to end well."

"And that ended well?"

"It always ends well if we get to go home," he said.

The gravity of that statement sat with me for months. It was their unofficial credo. Sergeants said it to lieutenants, and officers said it to me. The mantra "always go home" distilled the complexity of their job. It reinforced that in their line of work, anything can happen, any day, any time, to any one of us.

We parted ways at midnight without much talk, and when I got back to the center and hung up my bulletproof vest, I, too, thought, "I got to go home." I thought about all the people who had died over the course of the day. I wished them a smooth transition and favorable rebirth as I got into bed. *My day will come also*, I reminded myself, *maybe even tomorrow.*

I always try to go to Food for Less during the off-traffic hours, but in L.A., I've yet to figure out exactly when that is. This morning the place was packed, and a fight erupted in frozen foods when a man and woman had words over the last two Klondike bars. The woman wanted both and clutched the packs against her chest while she argued. I kept on toward the pet aisle.

When I came to where the cat food is, I stood looking at an empty shelf. A feeling of frustration yawned inside me. Sold out. And then I realized that almost all the shelves were empty. Apparently, a truck had skipped delivery for some reason, and as humans do, people had turned into churning animals. Nothing brings out greed like a shortage, and Food for Less looked a bit ransacked. The last loaf of rye bread sat open, bread crumbling out onto its vacant rounder. There were mostly empty refrigerators, and people pushed their carts wearing frowns. I checked for the peppermint guest candies for the zendo, but those were sold out too. So were my chocolate cupcakes, and toilet paper. Thankfully, the cat litter was in stock, but when I got to checkout, there were only two registers open, and the lines went deep into the aisles. It was just one of those uphill days, and the people who couldn't accept it looked crazier than the rest.

I had a noon meeting with the building and safety inspector from the city and didn't want to be late, so I gave up and lugged the cat litter back to the shelf and went to the car empty-handed. On the way out, I got trapped in the parking lot. A stalled car blocked an exit. Tension grew, people were laying on their horns, it was close to ninety-seven degrees, and no cars were moving. I thought of the Klondike bars melting in the lady's back seat. Only in L.A. can you have gridlock in a parking lot, a good reminder of our interconnectedness.

I got back to the center at 12:06 and a stout balding man stood on the porch, clipboard in hand. Carl, a resident with disabilities, was talking his ear off about monster trucks.

I climbed the steps. "Sorry I'm late, the traffic was horrible."

The inspector gave me the once over and clicked his pen in and out a few times. "No problem."

Carl followed me inside as I retrieved the residential keys. "Can we start with my room?" he said. "I'm in house 3!"

I looked at the building inspector.

"It's probably best to just start here; it's easiest to work top to bottom," he said, fanning his flushed face with the paperwork.

Reverend Shanti, I, and one other monk lived in the zendo. It passed inspection with flying colors except for some storage boxes in the attic that were deemed a fire hazard. I didn't know who owned the boxes but suspected it was the hoarder from one of the other houses.

We moved down the block systematically, and although we'd posted tenant notices about the inspection, most of the rooms looked as though the occupants had forgotten. Carl tagged along with us, touching every tree trunk on the sidewalk, counting them up. He'd come to the center about four years earlier on his twenty-first birthday when his foster parents were jailed. I felt sadness for him. He had the kind of mental disability that kept him at a child's intellect but gave him the awareness to know it. He lived on bananas, Altoids and Dr. Pepper and was employed through a public program picking up trash at the airport. His case worker was a big help to him and us.

Carl turned to the inspector. "Can we do my room next? I wanna show you my room."

Carl was the best kind of compassion practice. "We'll be over in a bit, Carl," I said. "Go get your room ready," and he raced off mimicking a monster truck as he climbed the stairs into his house.

The inspector looked at his paperwork.

"Seems like you all just had an inspection last year. We got a complaint?"

"A tenant called you guys," I explained. "He'd only been here a month, and when it came time to pay the rent, he refused, insisting we weren't up to code."

The inspector scanned the paperwork. "Not enough bathrooms?"

"I don't know the details, but he left in the middle of the night and took every light bulb in the house with him."

The inspector shook his head. "Hope you guys replaced those."

When we came to Carmine's room, I was a bit nervous, as she was a clinical hoarder.

"Guess she forgot we were coming," I said uncomfortably as we stood in the center of her room, ankle-deep in white plastic grocery bags. They were all tied at the handles and stuffed with stuff. They'd been arranged in piles and columns, creating a small, knee-high maze complete with aisles to the bed, window, and dresser. It was surreal and conjured the set of a low-budget snow castle film.

"It's compulsive," I said, stating the obvious.

He took out his point-and-shoot camera and popped off a wide shot of the room. "She can't even see what's in the bags," the inspector said. "She can't even see what she's saving. I don't get it."

"Maybe it's good we don't understand," I said.

But that was only partly true; although I couldn't understand the behavior, I could clearly understand the motivation. Carmine lived heavily snagged in the silly string of desire and attachment. The Buddha likened this phenomenon to drinking salt water: the more you drink, the thirstier you get.

"Hey, guys." Carmine appeared in the doorway dressed in her Whole Foods work apron. She was in her early thirties and looked like you'd find her in a yoga magazine.

"Hey, Carmine, we'll be outta here in just a sec."

"No rush, I'm gonna make lunch," she said, and off she went.

When we got to Ananda Hall, Carl ran out with a cold Dr Pepper for the inspector.

"My room's ready! Come see. I made you a present."

The inspector took the soda. "Thanks."

Carl lived on the third floor. It was an attic that had been renovated into a bedroom. He was allowed to live with us only because he was scared to death of appliances and things with an on/off switch. He avoided the stove, clothes iron, and garbage disposal, but thankfully didn't have a problem with the shower.

Carl's room was always changing; he collected things from the airport, the bus, the sidewalk. His case manager visited once a week, and if something seemed inappropriate or unsanitary, she came back while he was gone and cleared most of it out. The weird thing was Carl never seemed to notice; it just gave him something to do when he had to start from scratch all over again.

Today, the room looked pretty good. A few Oreo cookies lined the windowsill. He'd made them into little crabs using Altoids for eyes and crooked drinking straws for the legs. His walls were covered with crayon drawings. His case manager never pulled these down, and most of the drawings depicted airplanes and people who lived at the center. There was one of Shin in her nun's robe; he'd added yellow light all around her after she died. He pointed to the one he'd drawn of me. "It's Special K!" he said. Then he presented the inspector with a drawing of a stout man in a hat with a clipboard. It read "welkom" in Carl's scrawl across the bottom.

The inspector genuinely smiled. "Thanks. I like the hat you gave me."

Carl grinned in his earnest way. "Are the houses falling?"

"No, the houses are fine," he said.

"Promise? Promise me the house is OKAY!" Carl had gone from zero to ten on the hysterical meter, which didn't often happen. The inspector shot me a glance, which sent terror running through Carl. He jumped under the covers of his twin bed and crawled head first toward the foot of it.

"Carl," I said walking to his bed. "It's okay. Everything's okay."

He started crying.

"You can't stop it from falling! You can't!" he sobbed, and then he bolted out from under the covers, into the hall, and down two flights of stairs.

I stepped to the window and waited. "He'll be okay," I said as he popped full speed out into the backyard like a marble. I was reminded of "anicha," the Pali word for impermanence. It was one of the three marks of existence, and even though Carl had the brain of a child, he knew things that we, with our fully functioning brains, tried to forget.

IBMC passed the inspection just fine. The inspector left with a handshake, his Dr Pepper, and the drawing Carl made, plus a smile.

The following week, I showed up for my chaplain's shift at the police station and was assigned to ride along with Officer Lambert, who of course hadn't been told in advance. When we were introduced, he was getting into the squad car. He wasn't happy about the news and huffed and puffed, shuffling his things from the front seat into the trunk to make room for me. I imagined that if I'd shown up to do a dharma talk and there was some stranger following my every move onstage, I might be a bit annoyed too.

Lambert was a hard faced, wrinkled brow, "no nonsense" kind of guy, the sort of cop you'd hate to have pull you over, but the kind you'd definitely want to have looking for your abducted kid. There was something to his intensity that didn't seem so healthy, but I couldn't quite tell if it was anger or just an overly heightened sense of integrity.

As he moved the last of his belongings to the trunk, he gave it a hard slam, bouncing the car on its shocks. "How many shifts have you done?" he asked.

"Just one, with Officer Devon."

"And you're on the full twelve hours?"

I nodded, which meant a 3 a.m. wrap.

"I see." Lambert got into the car and mechanically tested the radio, siren, and computer system. "Officer Devon," he said. "Now there's a real piece of work. Forget anything he told you and pretend to know nothing."

"If there's one thing I know for certain," I said with a small smile of camaraderie, "it's nothing."

He looked at me with mixed eyes; I couldn't translate. In fact, I could almost never tell what any of the police officers thought about anything. They were always taking in information—verbal, nonverbal, situational, factual—and critically processing it instantaneously. And they did it all without an ounce of emotional rapport. It was an art form and an important part of what kept them "going home."

Lambert drove at the exact posted speed limit at all times.

"How long you have you been on the force?" I asked.

"Thirty years."

"All in Garden Grove?"

"Yep."

"Jeez, you must have seen a lot."

He said nothing for the next two hours as we patrolled residential roads and back alleys. He knew the city like his own house. We pulled off patrol into the courthouse parking lot, and that's when the downpour started.

"You can stay in here and not move a muscle," he said, "or I can lock her up and you just wait outside the courthouse."

I glanced at the streams of water running down the windshield and the trees swaying in the high winds. "I'll just stay in here if that's okay?"

"Okay, don't leave and don't touch anything," he said, slamming the door like an exclamation point. He walked slowly toward the courthouse in the heavy rain like some android from *Blade Runner*.

I liked being in the squad car alone. I looked around and thought about Marconi, Steve Jobs, and Ted Nugent. The dispatch radio perched delicately in its cradle, the database computer fit neatly on a tray between the seats, and the gun rack lived behind my head. A steel box was welded to the floorboard and held the ammunition. The red throw switches for Code 3 lights and sirens reminded me of the hazard lights in my father's Buick.

He was a traveling salesman and a standup comedian and did the best he could at being a father, which counts. I am the oldest of four. I have one sister, Wendy, and two brothers, Bob and Hunter. We moved around a lot growing up. I was born in Iowa in 1949, and when I was five, we moved to Phoenix, Arizona. There we stayed for nine years until my parents split. Phoenix wasn't great. It's where I fell out of a tree and broke both legs, one arm, and cracked five vertebrae. The injuries required a large back brace for many months, and I was held back from my first year of high school. I spent three months in traction and couldn't get out of bed. A nurse would come a few times a week to check on me, and she finally padlocked my brace on, because she knew that I had been taking it off at night to get comfortable. That was the sixties; things were different then.

So entering my teen years, I became significantly depressed about missing school and being relegated to bed. My mom tried everything to cheer me up, which included surprising me with a pet spider monkey, who I named Trevor.. Unfortunately, the monkey turned out to be a bit malicious or disturbed. One minute he'd be fine and cuddly, and the next he'd go into a tirade and start peeing everywhere. I don't really blame him; he was pent up in my room right alongside me. The nurse was worried that Trevor would cause an infection, plus when people came to visit, they'd stay only a short time because it smelled so bad. So

Trevor was with us for only a few weeks, and then he had to go.

After I healed, my parents got divorced. Dad moved back to Milwaukee. Mom packed up our blue station wagon, along with Rusty, the dog, and moved us all to San Diego. For a year we were happy, until she was diagnosed with uterine cancer. So we packed up the car again and moved to Milwaukee to be close to her parents for support. They helped her during the surgery and recuperation; she came through everything okay, thankfully.

When she was back on her feet, she wanted to return to Southern California, so she moved the family, minus me, out to Malibu. I moved in with Dad, and after high school, with his encouragement, I attended a local city college for a semester before I knew it wasn't for me.

Dad was a World War II veteran and had attended Iowa State University with help from the GI Bill. He graduated with a degree in speech therapy but never used it. When we lived in Phoenix, he was a sales manager with Standard Oil, and while the job supported our family, working for a corporation wasn't Dad's speed. That's when he started doing comedy. Somehow, he swung a regular gig on *The Wallace and Ladmo Show*, a local Phoenix TV children's program. He'd make guest appearances for the broadcast doing three-to-four-minute bits. He loved it.

After the divorce, he moved back to Milwaukee and took a traveling sales job with Paymaster, a company that made fraud-detecting check cashing machines. He could sell anyone anything, and in my freshman year of high school, he even managed to sell my girlfriend's family a Paymaster machine. The job kept him on the road, mostly traveling through the Midwest. He thrived on the flexible lifestyle and sold lots of machines. I think he liked the freedom it allowed.

Eventually the Paymaster job morphed into his own eccentric sales business. Somewhere along the way, he started stocking novelty items in the trunk of his car, things like astrological calendars, customizable matchbooks, and pens. He'd pull into a town, approach the local drugstore, and somehow he'd land a lot of his merchandise on their shelves. If he were alive now, he'd probably have his own eBay store filled with eccentric gifts and strangely useful items.

Dad was boisterous and loud and took over most any conversation. So when my father started doing stand-up comedy, it wasn't a big surprise. And it worked well with his sales job. He would route his sales trips around open mic nights in various cities, so in a way he was "on tour" as a comic but also selling Paymaster machines. And the stand-up comedy was all his, a part of his life the family knew little about.

When he was at home, he had an odd obsession with recording the audio from TV shows onto cassettes. I'd often come home to find the television on with a tape player in front of it, recording. His archives were meticulously catalogued, but I never saw him listen to a single one. I think in his mind, "owning" the entire series of *The Mary Tyler Moore Show* somehow made him feel rich.

Toward the end of his life, I started being asked to do public speaking on Buddhism, and when he found out, he asked for a recording. "You got my genes, kid," was all he said. I think he meant it as a compliment; he thought of himself as being in show business. I guess he was, kind of.

After graduating high school, I got my first job at the Milwaukee County Mental Health hospital. I passed the test to become an attendant, and on my first day, I walked in on a patient drinking his urine from the specimen cup. All I could muster was, "I don't think you're supposed to be doing that." I knew that if I worked that job long, I would become mentally ill too. So after a few months I quit, left Milwaukee for good, and joined Mom and the rest of my family out in Malibu. I've been in Southern California ever since.

Officer Lambert had been inside the courthouse for over an hour, and I couldn't see much through the blurry wet windshield except that night had come. The only entertainment was the sudden red brake lights of the cars as the drivers saw our patrol car sitting there.

Being in a cop car is a bit like being in a monk's robes: your presence in unignorable. Even though most people have no idea what my robes represent, they often avoid eye contact and put their back to me wherever possible.

When Officer Lambert returned, he opened the door and immediately did a visual check of the car, ending with a once over on me.

"It smells like breath in here," he said, cranking the AC. "Sorry."

Lambert did everything with an undertone of overexertion. "Took longer than anticipated," he said. It was about 7 p.m. "You hungry?"

Before I could say, "Heck, yes, I'm starving," the radio came alive, dispatching us to do a welfare check on an elderly man who ended up being fine. The man was in his 90s, and angry with his daughter for giving him one of those cognitive brain game books for elderly people. Although it was a gift, it had made him feel inept, so he refused to call her back. She lived a few hours away and called the police when she couldn't get hold of him.

"Slow night," Lambert said.

"Fine by me, glad there's nobody in trouble."

"There's always trouble somewhere," he said. "It's just not making its way to the surface is all."

I looked at him, sensing the profundity of what he'd said. It had some dharma to it. It reminded me that the seeds of ignorance and delusion are carried deeply within us, and have the potential to take root at any time.

By 9 p.m., the rain had dwindled to a drizzle, and he hadn't brought up dinner again. We pulled to the side of a residential street and camped out within sight of a stop sign. It took about thirty seconds for a driver to blow right through, and Lambert flashed the lights and the red Mercedes pulled over.

"Just stay in the car for these," he said.

I thought about my breath and cracked the window.

I'd always wondered if the police targeted certain cars for traffic tickets, like more expensive ones, but after an hour and a half and seven tickets, I realized there was no forethought for Lambert. When a driver ran the stop sign, he pulled them over. Simple. No matter what. And they got a ticket, no matter what.

Except for the last one he stopped. Around midnight, a rusted old Nissan Sentra rolled through the stop sign just like everyone else. Officer Lambert did his usual thing, but when he climbed back into the car, he looked rattled. He watched them drive away and pulled out a stick of gum.

"That lady," he said, "she had the skinniest, palest little child I've ever seen. It was so sick."

I shifted in the seat, giving him a moment.

"They were coming home after three weeks at the cancer center. Their insurance had run out."

He stared out the windshield. It was the stillest I'd seen him all night. He wasn't chewing his gum, wasn't scanning the surroundings, wasn't working; he just sat there. He was feeling.

"I let 'em go with a warning," he said finally.

"I think that probably helped them out a great deal, sir," I said.

He looked down at his ticket book and thumbed its corner. "In thirty years, I've let seven people out of tickets."

A car ran the stop sign in front of us. He let out a tired exhale and started the car. "Sick kids," he said. "How are we supposed to be happy and joyful and filled with smiles in a world where a little kid is that sick?"

"I don't know," I said.

He raised a pointed brow.

"I wish I had a better answer," I said. "There's nothing pretty about getting sick, growing old, and death. Especially if you're a kid. At least you looked right at it. Most people don't. It makes the good in life seems better if you acknowledge all the hard stuff too.

He stared at me.

"I just try to comfort people. I was told that chaplains are an expression of kindness," I said.

He shook his head and dropped the car in drive. "I'm hungry. How 'bout you?"

It was almost 11 p.m.

"Very," I said.

"Do you have a special diet, kosher or something?"

"No, just go wherever you wanna go. I'm good with anything except B-B-Q."

"Welcome to Subway," the sandwich girl said.

We eyed the sandwich parts.

Lambert got a hot chicken sandwich and I got a salad, grabbed some napkins, and sat at the table by the window.

"We're taking this to go," he said, walking past me and out the door.

It was about 11:30 p.m., and we drove across town to a large parking lot behind a bank. He grabbed his sandwich bag. "We don't eat in the squad car," he said, getting out.

The rain had started up again. Lambert went to the bank's back door and unlocked it, waving me through as he scanned the parking lot behind us.

I looked around inside. A few lights blinked on various machines.

"So the bank just gives you keys?"

"You should be transferred to investigation," he said, and gave a little laugh. We walked toward the tables and chairs in the lobby. "It's a win-win. We've got keys for various businesses, and they let us take breaks there and use their bathrooms."

"You just do their security then?"

"Well, it's not really for that, it's for the public good. How often do you see a police officer sitting down enjoying a meal in a restaurant?"

I thought.

"Maybe once in a while," he said, "like late night at Denny's. But it's really best if the public doesn't see us sitting around eating. It looks bad. For some reason when you carry a gun, you're expected to be working at all times. And even though we are, it may not look that way when we're putting food in our mouth. It's just the way it works. If we go into a restaurant, we may just put them out of business too. People feel uncomfortable around us, so we always get the food to-go and eat somewhere out of sight. But not in the car."

"Oh, that makes sense."

"And we get to use their bathrooms too. Much cleaner," he said, pulling out a bottle of hand sanitizer before unrolling his sub.

"Speaking of bathrooms, where is it?" I asked.

Officer Lambert got up and retrieved a key from one of the desk drawers. He walked me over to the glass gate that separates the back from the front, unlocked it for me, and pointed. "Down the hall."

I made my way past a few desks and slowed, glancing around. I saw big red buttons at hip level at every station. I thought those were just in the movies. There were steel pronged money counting machines, scrolling digital monetary conversion boards, yellow and red colored keyboards; it was all fascinating.

I went down the hallway and passed the steel vault door. I stopped to take a look at the spokes.

"DON'T TOUCH THAT!" he yelled from about fifty feet away.

I kept on going.

Returning to the table, I found Officer Lambert had switched our seats so his back was to the wall. I later found that lots of officers did this when sitting down (which rarely happens); most preferred to face the door, and on occasion, they'd ask me to sit next to them instead of in front of them if I blocked the view. It seemed like they should have been paid by the minute, as I never saw one of them come fully off duty for the entire twelve hours.

I sat down and realized Officer Lambert hadn't started eating. His sandwich lay neatly centered on the Subway wrapper, untouched. I nodded and took the lid off my salad.

"It's a strange feeling to be in a bank at night," I said.

Lambert was raising the chicken cheddar sub to his mouth when dispatch came over the radio. A possible burglary in progress, just a few blocks away.

We packed up, locked up, and arrived on scene in four minutes. A woman was peeking out the front window of a house and hurriedly waved us to the door. Lambert moved quickly, dodging his flashlight around as we approached.

The door flew open. "It's a man!" she said, clinching the side of her door.

Officer Lambert calmly stepped into her doorway.

"I'm Officer Lambert, and this is my partner, Kusala. What's your name, ma'am?"

"Heather."

"Okay, Heather, what happened?"

"I live alone, and I heard a noise on the side of the house. When I looked out the bathroom window, I saw a man lurking on the patio. Then he tried climbing the fence, but it was slippery from the rain. That's when I called the police. Then he came up to the front porch like he owned the place!"

She pointed to a yellow Adirondack chair and a crumpled can of Budweiser.

"I think that's his."

"What did he look like, and what was he wearing?"

"Blonde, dirty blonde short hair, red striped sweater, he had a brown backpack."

"Did you see any weapons?"

"No, but he had a white pointy thing in his hand. Like a prong."

"Okay, miss, we're going to have a look around for him and come back in a few minutes."

Lambert leaned against the stucco house and cranked his neck over the bushes. He sent his light searching through the branches.

"Go back to the car," he said to me.

Phew, I thought. I didn't want to get stabbed with a white prong thing.

"Get your flashlight so you can help me look," he added.

I jogged to the car and got it.

It was a big house, built about ten years earlier in one of those upscale tract home developments. We started our search on one side of the house; everything was dripping wet from the long rain. The tall grass sopped my socks and trouser legs.

At the back gate, we came upon another crumpled Budweiser can. Lambert picked the can up and threw it into a trashcan on the side of the house.

"I don't think this was attempted burglary," he said quietly. "I mean, he was wearing a red-and-white-stripped shirt. Sounds like a homeless guy."

Good point, I thought.

We searched the back and far side; the coast was clear. We went back to let Heather know.

"Whoever was here is definitely gone," said Lambert. "I don't think you were targeted or that he intended to break in. He was likely just collecting cans out of the garbage. Maybe homeless. We're going to patrol the area for at least the next hour looking for him. If you see him again, just give a call."

He handed her his card. "But for now just lock up the house and go to bed. Whoever he is, he's gone and probably wouldn't be able to find his way back here if he wanted to."

She looked relieved and thanked us.

We drove about five miles per hour for twenty minutes, up and down, back and forth. Lambert said nothing; he scanned like a cat. And then he hit the brakes and in a blink was out of the car, light in hand, heading toward a tan house with a steep roofline.

He perched his Maglite on his shoulder as I scurried up behind him, assuming the same position.

Lambert trained his light on a bush. "Hi, sir, what'cha doing in there?" he said kindly.

There was silence.

"Sir, can you step out here for a minute?"

I could see the man; he was pretty well tangled in the shrubs, and although fully illuminated, he sat crouched and frozen, eyes bulging like a spooked horse.

"We see you in there. Just come right on out, sir. We just need to talk to you."

The man blinked and scowled, refusing to move. Lambert stood in a slight squat, one hand holding the flashlight, the other resting on his belt by the taser and gun.

A light went on in the home, and a woman's face appeared in the window right above where the man was crouched. She clasped her hand over her mouth in horror as she saw what was happening.

"Ma'am," Officer Lambert said. "I'm a police officer. Everything's fine, but please step away from the window immediately." His delivery of "immediately" somehow made the word more real than I had ever heard.

She disappeared. "Hank! Hank!" she called from inside the house. "There's police outside and a man in our yard!"

"Okay, sir," Lambert said in an even voice. "We see you, and we need you to come right on out of there. We just need to talk to you, but we need you to do it now. I'm only going to ask this last time, or my partner and I are going to have to come in there."

The man moved nothing. Officer Lambert waited an uncomfortably long time, and the man finally stirred. His red striped sweater caught on every branch on his way out, and he took half the bush with him as he pulled free.

"Slowly, very slowly," Officer Lambert said.

The man uncurled and stood upright, leaning against the side of the house to steady himself.

"Sir, I need you to step away from the house."

The man pushed himself from the wall and stayed frozen, cornered. He raised his arm to block our lights from his eyes.

He was sopping wet. The cable knit sweater hung dirty and stretched in all the wrong places; his jeans were a dark, watered-down indigo. Grass and twigs clung to his entire body. I felt bad for the man.

"Stop that," he whispered. "Stop." The light was hurting his eyes, it seemed.

"Hands to the wall, sir."

The man docilely obeyed, and Lambert stepped close behind him and started patting him down.

"You okay, sir?" Lambert asked conversationally.

The man stood like a stiff wooden doll, teeth chattering.

Dangling off his belt loop by a leather rope was a large white oxen horn that looked like a movie prop, something a cowboy in a western would use to store his gun powder. A piece of leather covered the opening at the top.

"Any weapons on you, sir?" asked Lambert.

The man shook his head.

"What's in here?" Lambert asked, unsnapping the Oxen horn from his belt.

"Bernie."

The leather cover popped off easily. Lambert motioned for me to shine my light inside. A thin tail stuck up toward us, and at the other end was a clean little white lab mouse, burying its head in fear.

"Please," the man whispered, "stop."

Lambert lightly slid his hand from the man, letting him know the search was over.

The man exhaled a huge sigh of relief.

"Okay then," Lambert said, "just keep your hands on your head, and let's go have a little talk on the sidewalk."

"I'm scared."

"We're not here to hurt you. Just keep your hands on your head. Everything's okay."

"I have to go."

"We need to talk out front, sir.

Keep your hands on your head, and we're going to head straight across the yard to the car, okay?"

Lambert guided him from the lawn.

Once we were standing by the curb, Lambert asked him what he intended to do back there.

The man said he was trying to find an overhang to

sleep under. He spoke softly and rationally for a thin, tired, homeless man. He'd just come back from Afghanistan the year before.

"Do you have ID on you?"

"No, they stole my wallet. I can't sleep in the city; people mess with me there. Out here, nobody gonna rob me."

"I understand, but you see those people?" Lambert nodded up to the couple peering out their bedroom window at us. "You scare them when you sleep in their yard. And see all those people over there?" He nodded at the pajama crowd that now lined the sidewalks and porches up and down the block, watching. "You scare them too."

The man dropped his head and nodded.

"What's your name?"

"Tim."

"Now Tim, because all those people are watching, and because you've trespassed on these people's property, I have to put you in the car. They won't feel safe unless I take you on out of here, okay?"

For the first time, Tim raised his head and looked Lambert in the eye.

"Please, please, don't take me in. We'll never come here again. I swear."

The rapidity of his pleading took us both by surprise.

"I have to put you in the car, sir, I'm sorry."

Tim looked at me. "Please, I promise I won't come round again, I promise."

"This is Kusala," Lambert said. "He'll wait here with you while I go grab something, okay?"

Lambert walked past the car and across the street to a small public park. He headed toward a trashcan under a lamppost, removed the lid, pulled out the bag of trash, and set it on the sidewalk. Then he leaned into the can and came up with a roll of trash bags. He tore a fresh one free.

As Lambert spread the trash bag over the back seat of the patrol car, a creep of sad surrender crawled across Tim's face. If he'd been offered any way to die versus getting into that car, my guess is he'd have taken it. His eyes glassed over and watery tears filled them. I felt mine about to follow suit.

Lambert stepped closer to Tim and glanced back at the people in the window.

"I'm gonna come around behind you now and walk you to the car. You can take your hands off your head. Just put them behind your back till we get to the car, okay?"

Tim did as directed, looking like a soldier walking the plank. He got in. I got in. Lambert got in. As we pulled away, the rain started up.

The car smelled like urine and sadness.

Once we got out onto the main street, Officer Lambert motioned for me to hand his chicken cheddar sandwich through the glass window to Tim. We drove in silence as Tim tore bites off the sandwich like a starving animal. When we reached the southeast side of town, we parked on a residential street of low-income houses. Across the way was a twenty-foot barbed wire fence, the perimeter of a well-known golf course.

"Stay here," Lambert said to me.

He walked up to a large dilapidated house and knocked on the door. A man answered, and Lambert wiped his feet and went in.

Tim had fallen asleep after his last bite and now hung forward in his seatbelt like a tired toddler strapped in a car seat.

About ten minutes went by, and Lambert reappeared at the door with a heavyset man. They made their way to the car, and Lambert tapped on the glass, waking Tim before opening the door.

"You okay?" Lambert asked.

Tim was confused.

"Tim, my friend, you have very good luck," Lambert said. "This man here is named Eddie. He found you a bed in the shelter for tonight. They've got some clothes inside for you, some hot coffee, and in the morning, one of the advocates can help you start the process of getting your identification reissued."

Eddie and Officer Lambert flanked Tim as they helped him up the stoop and into the house.

Officer Lambert returned shortly and opened the back door.

"Where's the trash bag?" he asked.

"I threw it out," I said.

"Thanks," he said, getting back in.

We drove for the first few minutes in silence.

"How often do you do that?" I asked.

"That was the first," he said.

When Steve LaFond passed away, the chaplaincy program lost something for me. Steve was such a wonderful guide through the whole thing, and he was able to interpret the police officers for us. He showed us where the line was between us and them, and made me feel comfortable there. So when he was gone, I felt like our group had lost its translator. And I had something else to do; I wasn't sure what, but something always comes along that directs the next move. So after seven years, I left to make room for the next opportunity to serve.

Chapter 2
Lockdown, Contraband, and Springtime:
The Prison Year 1995

I took a few steps back to stay out of the way; never did I think I'd find myself there. The prison waiting room had an old beige linoleum floor, which met the old beige plaster walls without camaraderie. Five inmates dragged their mops about with practiced indifference; their tangerine jumpsuits jeered loudly against the drab walls. Every so often, our eyes would meet; I'd give a little nod or smile, and they'd just stare right through me like I was a windshield. A guard stood right outside the door.

It was my first time in prison, and although I was in a special waiting area reserved for volunteers, it didn't feel so special. I'd been there seven minutes, and I checked the clock habitually. The room was hot and growing more humid with every dunk of the mops.

Maybe if I'd been the kind of monk who sat reading long, dry scriptures or practiced daylong meditations, I wouldn't be here right now. I thought how fast life could change with a single phone call.

The day the phone rang, I'd been at my computer nursing a coffee and updating UrbanDharma.org.

"I'm calling for Kusala Bhikshu," a voice said.

"This is he," I said between sips.

"I'm Deacon Samanski from the Men's California State Correctional Facility.

I saw that *L.A. Times* article about you and thought you might be able to help us. We could really use someone like you up here."

"Where?"

"In the prison," he said.

A clink rang through the phone as I set down the coffee cup.

"We've got some Buddhist prisoners in here, and I'd really like to get someone who could work with them."

"How many Buddhists do you have in there?" I asked.

"I'm not sure, but we've got some in each yard. Yard four has the most, I think."

I paused, wondering how so many Buddhists ended up in prison. Last I checked, there was nothing illegal about the Four Noble Truths and the Eight-Fold Path.

"If you could commit to maybe once a week? Just come up, give a talk or whatever you'd like, maybe some meditation?"

"Are you downtown?" I asked.

"No, Lancaster," he said.

My inner Rolodex spooled.

"It's about an hour and a half north of L.A.," he said.

"That may be a bit of a challenge. I don't have a car."

"Oh, right. The article said you ride a motorcycle. You'll probably get here even faster, and it's a nice drive through the desert, lots of open space."

And just like that, so began a year-long commitment within the beige walls of the men's prison.

What Deacon Samanski hadn't said was it would be high desert motorcycle riding, so the cold was freezing, the hot was scorching, and the wind never stopped blowing. Once I saw a rolling torrent of wind gust across a field and knock a goat down to its little knees. The bike would often get hit the same way, and I'd find the bike switching lanes without warning. I wouldn't term it a "relaxing ride," though later I became grateful for the distance. It gave me time to decompress, and it kept the prison experience far from home, which turned out to be good.

The trek up to Lancaster was incredibly hot, and even though the robes of a monk provide a special kind of protection, that protection has no crossover value when it comes to motorcycle riding. So the robes traveled in my side bags, and I wore an old leather bomber jacket and blue jeans. During the summer, I baked on the ride, and every so often, the thought of spending the night in prison seemed more appealing than riding back down in the heat. If it weren't for the bodhisattva vows I'd taken, I'd have backed out of the whole thing, but vows are vows, and they inspire a level of dedication that only the taker of the vows understands.

I'd always wished my karma would have directed me toward the path of an arahant rather than a bodhisattva. The arahant path is streamlined and begins with self-discovery of the dharma (the teachings of the Buddha) followed by mastery and zap!—the ultimate truth of reality is realized. This realization is sometimes defined as the complete and total cessation of suffering, karma, and all future rebirths. An arahant never returns for another rebirth, and some days, especially on the hot ones riding toward the men's prison, I'd have been more than happy if this were my last lifetime.

But as it goes, my path sifted out to be that of the bodhisattva. The vows we take state our commitment to return lifetime after lifetime to help all beings find their way out of suffering. And although it's a clear-cut case of the infinitely impossible, it somehow gives life purpose, which feels more meaningful than just "go to work, pay the bills, go to bed, and repeat till death do us part." The bodhisattva vows are recited and renewed daily, which challenges a person to expand their limits of compassion, plus it keeps the mundane aspects of life—news, weather, sports—at bay.

For seven years, my only form of transportation was a motorcycle. I'd had a car up until the late 80s, but it broke down, and my insurance was about to expire. I tried to pull enough money together for a used car but had no luck. So one day on the bus, I looked out the window and saw someone riding a motorcycle. The sun was shining and the temperature was pleasant. I thought, why not? As a teenage, I'd had a 50 cc Honda scooter; I loved tooling around

Phenoix. I checked around and found that Mariner Suzuki was offering new and used motorcycles, some for less than $1,000. I had some credit left on my charge card, so I headed over.

It was a whole new world. They had everything: scooters, mopeds, and small, medium, and large motorcycles. Some had exposed engines, and some had so much chrome it was blinding. I explained my situation to a salesperson; she was sympathetic and suggested a few lower-end bikes, but none of them really spoke to me. She motioned to me to follow her outside, where they had some used bikes. As we walked around, I spotted the bike I wanted: a used Kawasaki Eliminator 250 cc, liquid-cooled, 33 horsepower, and a 6-speed transmission.

I pulled out my charge card, and $1,500 later, I was the owner. The dealership took two photos of me sitting on the bike, one for the dealership wall and one for me. I made my way off the lot and rode to the first gas station I could find to fill her up. It took 2.9 gallons.

The next chore was to get a motorcycle license. The dealership gave me a temporary license, which allowed me to ride in daylight hours, plus a booklet on moto rules of the road. A few months later, I took my riding and written tests and passed with flying colors. I was now an official motorcycle guy.

It took a while to feel comfortable in L.A. traffic. Everyone else was sitting inside a metal cage behind glass, and I felt like exposed soft-serve, like a target. But as the miles added up, so did my confidence. Eventually I felt safe getting from point A to point B, and on occasion, I'd even split lanes but didn't do that often. One wrong move and you're toast.

After the first 250 cc motorcycle, I moved up to a 550 cc Suzuki and then to an 800 cc Suzuki. I'm glad I started small; it was a slow process to build skill and confidence, but after seven years of riding in all weather conditions in L.A., and after doing my five-thousand mile trip to Wisconsin and back to visit the parents, I'd was seasoned.

"Kusala Bhikshu?" a baritone voice called out. A uniformed guard appeared in the doorway and came toward me, clipboard in hand. "You the monk?"

I was the only one in the room and also dressed in robes. "Yes," I said.

"I need your ID and keys, but that stuff"—he motioned to my motorcycle jacket, backpack, and helmet—"can't come in."

"Is there a locker or a desk I could—"

"Nope."

And then he just stood there, waiting for me to figure it out.

I looked around the waiting room as if someone were going to give me an answer, but the five men only mopped in silence.

"Put it in your car," he said.

"I ride a motorcycle."

"Put it in there then."

"In where?"

We stared at each other.

"It doesn't have a trunk," I said.

"Sorry, but that stuff can't come in."

The wind was relentless in the parking lot, and the bike now had a dusty brown finish. Flying dirt sandblasted my head as I strapped the helmet and bag to the handlebars with a bungee cord. The load dangled awkwardly, banging against the gas tank in the wind. I began to whisper the bodhisattva vow. "Sentient beings are numberless; I vow to save them all. Deluding passions are inexhaustible; I vow to end them all. Dharma gates are limitless; I vow to study them all. Buddha's way is supreme; I vow to attain it." Sometimes the recitation helped redirect my thinking away from old-fashioned complaining.

On the way back in, I asked the Buddha and bodhisattvas to protect the belongings; after all, it was the visitor's parking lot of a prison.

Deacon Samanski was waiting for me inside. "It's pretty windy out there, huh?"

"Yeah, it messed up my hair," I joked.

He chuckled and went on to say how grateful he was that I'd come. After he told me a little about what to expect, we started into the prison, following a guard down a long hallway toward a massive wall of black steel bars.

Midway, we stopped at a checkpoint where a female guard sat behind a pane of glass. It reminded me of a late-night gas station. She pushed a plastic bowl through a slit in the window.

"Keys, wallet, and change, please."

I emptied my pocket, and our trio continued on. The guard walked directly in front of us, and I couldn't help but watch his large wad of keys jangle like some Barney Fife prop. As we neared the wall of bars, a buzzer sounded, and the gate hinges creaked awake, slowly pulling to one side.

Deacon Samanski extended his hand. "Well, Kusala, I'm off to a meeting, but we're sure grateful. I know it's a heck of a trek."

"Always a pleasure to help," I said.

And with a handshake, nod, and smile, we parted ways.

The guard and I continued. As I stepped over the track of the lockdown gate, it felt like a precipice. The loud clank of the bars behind us sent a ripple of uneasiness through my gut. It was a bit like the movies, and the air felt stale and cooler. The guard and I walked onward toward a big steel door at the end of the hallway.

"So, what kind of monk are ya?" he said, giving my brown robes the once over.

"Buddhist," I said, with a tinge of pride.

"Geez, next they'll let astrologers start coming, too."

I laughed, and finally he did too. "Did Deacon Samanski go over the rules with you?"

I nodded but he reiterated them anyhow.

"Never have any items with you. Nothing. Nothing in pockets, socks, or underwear, and no food, pens, toothpicks, keys, pets, or identification. You can pick up your stuff at the same window on the way out."

With a loud racket of keys and a big shove, he opened the door to the outdoor courtyard. It was the size of a baseball field. The noontime sun blazed, and a sea of glimmering razor wire looped around the top of the chain-link fence. We walked at a fast clip as he began the tour.

"This is yard one and houses the least violent prisoners. Over there is yard four; it's maximum security. Yards two and three are everything in between. You're due in yard four, right?"

"That's what the deacon said," I gulped.

Each yard was similar in design, and between yards three and four stood a large Native American teepee and sweat lodge. It looked completely out of place, as if an installation from the Natural History Museum had fallen into the prison yard.

"Them Native Americans do their religion in there," the guard said.

As we walked on toward yard four, I could feel the eyes in the watchtowers tracking us. Between each yard, they'd buzz us in and out of the double gates.

"Pretty tight operation," I said.

"We're paid to keep it that way."

He pointed at a tan shoebox-shaped building. "That's the chapel."

We stopped at the yard sergeant's station to sign me in, and he radioed to have the Buddhist prisoners brought down.

"You're in the room over there." The guard motioned to a nondescript meeting room that could have been in any small business park in America. Then he pulled a small plastic box with a button from his belt and clipped it to my robe; it looked like a garage door opener.

"If anything goes left, just hit this and we'll be alerted,

but under no circumstances try and retrieve it by force if an inmate takes it from you."

"Okay," I said, without really thinking about what I'd just agreed to.

"And if there's a lockdown, just sit tight. You're safer where are you than anywhere else. They don't usually last too long, maybe a half hour or so. I'll be back in about ten minutes. I think there's eighteen who signed up."

"Sounds good," I said.

Inside the building were three meeting rooms and a chapel. The Buddhists had the smallest room, the Muslims met across the hall, and the Christians met in the chapel. The chapel was the only room that felt at all like a church, but like the teepee in yard three, it also had the feel of a museum installation. It was haunting. Nothing hung from the walls, and nothing loose lay about. There were no pictures of Jesus or Mary or any of the usual iconography, and aside from a few rows of mini pews and a heavy wooden pulpit, all it offered was a menial bookshelf in the far corner, filled with a litany of discourse, most of it Christian.

The light in our classroom was soft; the entire wall was lined with large banks of windows that overlooked the outdoor yards. I took in the scene. A few men ran circles on a dirt track; a few others were lifting weights while a small group sat on a grassy patch off to the side in handcuffs. Most of the men stood with their backs to the perimeter fence, surveying the yard, watching the comings and goings from a distance. I'm sure they knew I was watching, and I'd soon understand that most of the time, they knew everything about the unimportant. It was all they had; it was all they were allowed to have.

I was standing in our room, looking out the window, when the prisoners filed in silently. Nobody spoke, nobody made loud footsteps; there was just the quiet scuff of slipper shoes trodding the short pile carpet. They sat in the classroom chairs, but not without careful consideration of neighboring seatmates. It was my first introduction to the rudiments of prison culture, and I would come to learn that there was an unspoken hierarchy and etiquette that took into account "male wives" and warring factions. It was astounding that a group of humans with so little personal freedom could form a social structure so similar to that of the outside world.

As for the prisoners, I had no desire to know what they were in for. In fact, I tried to avoid learning anything, for neutrality's sake. I also tried not to ask "How's it going?" because the answer was pretty obvious. I had no expectations of them or of myself. I was there to talk dharma, and if I transmitted one tiny thing that helped even one of them to suffer less, it was a good day at the office. But what I didn't count on was that these beings, these maximum-security beings, embodied some of the most profound ties to human suffering I'd yet to encounter. And to spend time in a room with that suffering gave me a completely new understanding of compassion.

I sat down in the single chair at the front and started with a short introduction about myself. Then I suggested we go around the room so they could do the same.

There were a few Asians who didn't speak much English but had a devotional practice, burning incense as an offering because they knew that if they prayed to the Buddha, it was better than not praying to the Buddha. A few had a martial arts background, a handful had meditation experience, and one or two landed on the sign-up sheet for lack of anything better to do. I wasn't surprised that there wasn't much formal dharma knowledge among them, reconfirming my hope that most practicing Buddhists don't end up in prison.

I began with my usual lead: "Let's start with a few minutes of meditation." About one minute in, I lifted my eyes to see how the group was doing. Not a single man had his eyes closed. They sat erect and attentive; some watched out the window, and some stared at the heads in front of them, surveying all that could be surveyed. A few watched the Muslims through the glass in the other room, and others sat with the stature of a bodyguard. I realized closing their eyes was never an option. Their survival depended upon an awareness of their surroundings at every moment. In a way, it was mindfulness, but without the good parts.

I scanned the group; their deep, dead eyes stared back at me, their postures loaded with discernible volatility, their lips lifeless with indifference. A sharp feeling of unease hung in the air. I was calibrating the extensive amount of suffering that filled out the room, and I understood that these men were far more familiar with suffering than I could ever be.

What was missing from these beings was the spiritual light of empathy and compassion. Whatever they'd done to land in maximum security had everything to do with an extreme connection to the three kleshas: greed, hate, and delusion. It wasn't until months later, when thumbing through some literature, that I realized this was quite literally the hell realm. This was the anger, terror, and claustrophobia depicted in the Wheel of Life, a painting that can be seen in most Mahayana Buddhist temples that shows a pig, a snake, and a bird eating one another's tails in the endless cycle we call samsara. It's the term to describe the cycle of never-ending suffering of sentient beings.

It was no wonder I felt so little life in that room. These beings were trapped, and although I wasn't going to make a huge difference, if I could offer some sort of teaching that lessened their suffering, it'd be time well spent.

"Let's start with any questions?" I said.

A skinny man raised his hand. "Is it hard living in a meditation center? I mean, is it like here a little? Rules and stuff?"

"Every well-lived life usually has some boundaries more or less. For me, the vows gave me fewer options and turned my life as a monk into a lifestyle. Having fewer choices simplifies things, which brings a certain clarity for me."

"Are women allowed in your center?"

"We do have both men and women living there, but in Asia, that would not be the case; monks and nuns would be separated. At my center, we also have both lay people and monastics living there. I don't think it makes a big difference, because I've found that if you have humans living together, monastics or not, men or women, it's always a challenge. But that's the point: we get a chance to use the teachings in our lives."

A man blurted, "What do they wear, the women?"

I paused, feeling the group's heightened attentiveness

Every man was hanging on the words I was about to say, just waiting for me to describe what the women wore. "They dress mostly covered, long sleeves, long pants." I decided to throw in "turtlenecks" just for fun. "Out of respect for the monastic community, showing a lot of skin there isn't common." The paint of disappointment rolled over the inmates' faces.

"You all don't have sex, do you?" asked a man I would come to know as Cesar.

"No."

"Man, how do you guys do that? I could never do that." He shifted in his seat, crossing his arms. "I mean, why sign up for that?"

"Well, the idea of monks not having sex is an old one, and comes right from the Buddha himself. If you have sex, you're going to have kids sooner or later. Then you have to feed them, make a home for them, and maybe even send them to college. Having sex and having a family is what most folks want, what most folks end up with, but for a monk or a nun, they just want to be free."

A man raised his hand and said matter-of-factly, "How come I was born with a strong desire to rape women while other people aren't?"

"It's not that mysterious, actually. From a Buddhist perspective, that's just desire, only yours is really strong. Almost all men and women want to have sex, they think about having sex, do anything it takes to have it. The universe taps us on the shoulder until we have sex. It takes a lot of discipline not to have sex every time you want to. It's our biological job to make sure we have enough humans to populate the world. We are up to seven billion, I think.

If you can figure out how not to have sex, the world becomes a very different place, as do all your relationships. There is a level of freedom that comes when that's not in play."

This explanation was met with complete blankness.

"Would you guys like some Buddhist books in here?" I asked, pivoting.

Nobody raised a hand. I would also come to learn that prisoners rarely share opinions if asked to.

"I'll bring some next time," I said.

In the parking lot, a beach ball–sized tumbleweed had snagged on the bike's engine block. I set it loose, watching it roll toward the razor wire fence. My thoughts were churning, trying to make sense of the day.

How could beings become so lightless? Was it their karma? Was it environmental? Would being locked up give them a fair chance to shift perspectives?

Ironically, I realized that incarceration actually allowed for an accelerated path to wisdom if they so wanted. They were free from distraction, and all their basic needs were met. In many ways, the prison provided more creature comforts than a monastery: Their beds were off the floor; they received three meals a day rather than two; and they had all of their medical needs covered on site, twenty-four hours a day. They actually had an unusual opportunity to focus and cultivate their minds. Funny how life works.

It's been said that the human path to liberation needs only a breathing body, a seeking mind, and kindness. It has little to do with circumstances and requires only the discipline of meditation and exposure to the dharma. The mere fact that these men signed up for the teaching was progress itself and could be one of the many dharma gates in their path leading to the cessation of suffering.

I started the bike, zipped up my mind on the subject, and began to recite the loving-kindness mantra. The ride home was beatific. The road and bike clung together in perfect unity, and I sank into the billowing storm clouds gathering at the horizon. They existed without thought, hung without motive, and were imbued with an orange-gray light, which signaled the coming of fall.

As I rode, I found myself thinking of the path that led me to IBMC and to my ordination as a monk. I started to mature out of my rabble-rousing phase when I was around twenty-six.

I'd carved out a decent living and had a small apartment in West L.A. I managed a boutique in Westwood Village, which was the hip part of town in the '70s. Seybold was open from 10 a.m. till midnight, serving both celebrities and university students. We sold women's clothing and shoes. It was a two-story affair with French provincial decor, boasting orange and yellow carpet, rock and roll music, and brimming ashtrays. In some ways, it was almost like working at a party.

I had girlfriends, a car, and guy buddies, but something fundamental was missing. I suffered from a sense of vacancy and meaninglessness and often found myself distraught when I was supposed to be having a good time at parties or with friends. I became more aware of my own mortality and took to going to the gym. I gained twenty-five pounds of muscle from daily protein shakes, and my ego gained the same. Yet contentment still eluded me. Looking back, I realize it took only a few years to change my body, but changing my mind would turn out to require a lifetime of practice.

I remember taking psychology at a local college to try to understand myself and the world, but I ended up dropping out. I preferred the challenge of self-learning, and the traditional model of college teaching never stimulated me. I was always the sort of student who couldn't learn just because I was told to; I had to have an interest in the subject in order to retain anything. But I've always had an affinity for a good library. My bachelor's degree in Buddhist Studies came from passion; I finally found something I connected with academically.

When I was around twenty-eight, I started frequenting the Bodhi Tree Bookstore, where I found Eastern philosophy ideas about death and life challenging and truthful. I read a few books on alternate consciousness and checked out a meditation book at the library and started giving it a try on my own. While self-leaning works for lots of things, I soon realized that my uncontrollable mind couldn't train itself to meditate. I would need formal training. So one night, while pumping gas, I found IBMC.

It was raining, and as I stood there watching the gas pump ticker roll, I noticed the yellow pages hanging inside a phone booth just a few steps away. I ducked in and half-heartedly checked to see if there was a meditation heading. There was, but the list was short. Some place called Harriet's Hideaway was first, followed by IBMC. There were also three temples listed with long Asian names, and I wasn't Asian. The International Buddhist Meditation Center seemed the only option.

I put a quarter in the phone, and the following Monday found myself looking for parking in front of 928 South New Hampshire Street. It was early spring, and already dark at 7 p.m. When I pulled in front of a yellow residential house, I looked back at the paper I'd written the address on, sure this wasn't the place. I'd expected lava lamps in the window and the smell of patchouli, but there was nothing—no IBMC signage, no hippies playing flutes or hacky sack, no waft of sage.

What I saw was just a hundred-year-old Craftsman style house with a small porch and a tiny sign that read "Quan Yin House."

I stood on the dimly lit porch looking through the screen door, half-expecting to be greeted by a Korean with a shotgun. Instead, a group of Caucasian monks rounded the hallway's corner. The monk at the rear of the line paused and looked in my direction, waving for me to come in. They began with an introductory course on meditation, a long diatribe that was more like a biology class, with discussions of the diaphragm, and breathing past your lungs. When we finally got to the meditation, I couldn't even think about the breath. My knees hurt, my back needed support, and my mind was agitated. Why did I think this would be the answer? I was in the wrong place, doing the wrong thing. Just as I was about to leave, the gong rang, and a teacher appeared. He gave a talk about esoteric but interesting things, and I began to realize that meditation was going to be a key component in my evolution. All told, the session was two hours long and painful, but I went back. From that point on, things unfolded gradually. It was more of a process than an event that brought me to taking monastic vows.

The name given to me when I took the five precepts and three refuges was Kusala, which means skillful. And it's not because I am; it's because I'm not. My first teacher, Shinzen said, "It's what you need to become, and every time someone says your name, it will remind you to be skillful when responding." My second name is Ratana. A monk's second name is traditionally based on one's primary teacher; mine was Dr. Ratanasara. My third name is Karuna. A monk's third name is taken from one's ordaining monastic, which in my case was Reverend Karuna Dharma. So my full ordination name is Kusala Ratna Karuna Bhikshu, which translates to Skillful Jewel of Compassion. The Bhikshu at the end just means "monk." This system of naming ordainees enables one to trace a monk's lineage, i.e., to see who came from what teacher and what place of ordination. In the West, monks often add "Reverend" in front of it all, so that when we are doing interfaith work, other clergy members know we are fully ordained.

Becoming a full monk requires taking a series of vows over several years. The first step is to become an official lay Buddhist. This happens when you take the three refuge vows and hold the five precepts for one year. After that year, your teacher reviews your conduct and study and allows you to become a postulant, which means you hold the eight precepts. One year after that, you go on to become a novice monk, holding the ten precepts and the novice monk vows. The next step, to full ordination, depends on which tradition you are participating in. Theravada monks take over two hundred vows, and Mahayana monks—my tradition—take over three hundred vows. At our center, we hold the full ordination for five years; it's an apprenticeship. After five years, you receive a red robe, which means you are authorized to teach or to start your own center. I received my robe in September 2002.

So becoming a fully ordained monk is no small commitment. And taking the vows changed me. Forever. It redirected my motives in a way that gave my life meaning. The vows required me to help people, and to examine my own mind, self, and world. Every day. Those were my goals. Some people view the monastic restrictions as harsh, but I've actually found them to be quite freeing. If you take your vows seriously, there are only a few avenues to travel down, so things get much simpler, clearer. The ordination study, the lead-up, and the taking of the vows is different for everyone, but all I can say is that the older I get, the more grateful I am to have walked this path, and grateful for the tradition, and grateful for all the people who have helped and continue to help me along the way.

On the second week, I set off for the prison with an array of Buddhist books. Most of them came from IBMC's book donation room, though a few had been donated by members of the sangha. I'd packed the motorcycle's saddlebags carefully, wrapping the books in towels; as a monk, I'd been taught the importance of treating the dharma teachings with respect. The books added significant heft to the bike, and after nearly getting blown into oncoming traffic by a sudden wind gust, I was forced to pull to the side of the road and rearrange them, evening out the weight distribution for safety's sake.

When I arrived in Lancaster, the prison was on lockdown. Lockdowns were usually caused by an inmate disturbance, a fight, a death, or a major security breech. Every lock in the prison could be closed with the push of a single button. Anyone on the inside was locked in wherever they stood, and any inmates who were outdoors in one of the yards were required to drop down into a sitting position. Anyone waiting to get in stayed waiting. I was told the lockdowns usually lasted only around twenty minutes, so I took a seat in the volunteers' waiting room.

I looked at the beige walls and the beige floor. The only decoration in the room was an aged patchwork-quilt pillow on one of the chairs. A long, scroll-like poster on the wall listed a few security recommendations and tips for prison etiquette. A barren beige countertop wrapped the perimeter of the room veranda-style, and on it sat a murky Tupperware cake cover housing a few blurry, breaded snacks. After an hour and a half—and after I'd digested the driest mini-doughnut ever—I asked if I could at least leave the books for the chapel bookshelf before heading home. The answer was a simple "no," so I drove back to L.A.

I gave it another shot the following week. When the prisoners arrived in the chapel building, it was a whole new crew except for two Asian men, but they just sat in the back, holding space in the vacuum of their language barrier.

"So, I've brought some books." I pulled one from the pile on the chair beside me. "They'll be on the bookshelf in the chapel and are free for the taking."

A man in the front row got up to peruse; I held up a copy of the Dhammapada.

"This one's really good. It's not the easiest read, but it's got a lot of good dharma, and it's the first Buddhist book I ever read."

A man in the back row showed the tiniest flash of interest.

Then we went around the room again for introductions. A few of the men started talking about why they were in prison, and one guy said he was sure he was going to hell.

"Well," I said, "we have thirty hells and thirty heavens in Buddhism, so you may end up in a better hell than most, if that's any consolation."

The man didn't smile at my joke; none of them did. Talk of hell wasn't what they wanted to hear; they were already living it.

"So," I said, "are there any questions to start us off?"

A man raised his hand. "How come the Buddha always looks stoned? He don't seem happy. In every statue, he's just like super zoned out."

"At lease he's not hanging all bloody on a cross," the guy next to him said.

I cleared my throat. "While you're right about Christian iconography, it's only one depiction of Christ; he's also portrayed as being very vibrant in a lot of pictures. But I agree about the bloody cross thing; it's a bit harsh. As for the Buddha, no one really knows what he looked like. The first image was made hundreds of years after the Buddha died. For that matter, nobody knows what Christ looked like either. Maybe the artist who first drew the Buddha was trying to show what inner peace and calm might look like on the outside."

A wiry man asked, "Are you guys vegetarian?"

"Well, the early Buddhists were beggars; they ate what was offered. The old saying 'Beggars can't be choosers' may have come from monks. The later schools of Buddhism grew their own food, and because they took a vow of not killing, they became vegetarians. The Buddhist monks and nuns of Tibet eat meat because it is very hard to grow vegetables there. Sometimes where you live has a lot to do with what you eat, no matter what the rules are."

A man named James started in. "Hey, Holmes, any chance you could talk to the warden about getting us veggie meals? Maybe find some religious loophole or something? I'd kill for fresh tomatoes."

"Sorry," I said, "but I don't have any clout in here. There are advocates for that kind of thing, I think. Maybe talk to them."

James protested my response by kicking the chair in front of him, jolting the chair's occupant. The man's eyebrows twisted into a wrinkled wad as he turned around. The room went still. Even the Muslims in the next room looked in our direction, sensing something.

"I'm not here to talk about your diet," I said, "I'm here to talk about your mind!" The sternness of my voice surprised us all. James shrank a bit in his chair and crossed his arms like a teenager.

"Are there any more questions?" I asked. "Maybe related to the dharma?" There was a long pause.

"Okay then, take a book on your way out if you want."

As the men filed past me, James stared straight ahead. The man in the back row who'd shown an interest in the Dhammapada was last and paused to pick up the book.

"Take it," I said. "If you don't like it, just bring it back."

He stared at the cover as if it were a framed picture of his mother, and he ran a thumb over the title. Then he handed it back. "Seeing as I can't read, it best be given to someone else, I think."

I gave a slight nod and took the book. His eyes dropped to the floor as he turned to catch up with the other men.

"Here," I said, "take this. It's a Buddhist comic book, mostly pictures. And I've got a lot of recorded teachings on tape I could bring. Come next time, and I'll have 'em."

He glanced over his shoulder and gave me a look of silent thanks as he rounded the corner. I never saw him again.

On the way home, just outside of Lancaster, I stopped at an In-N-Out Burger, which began a ritual. I liked getting a small order of fries and a chocolate shake; it gave me a chance to collect my thoughts and get some calories before the long ride home. It was somehow an oddly rejuvenating act. I saw kids smiling with kid meals, mischievous coworkers poking fun at one another, couples sharing milkshakes. It reloaded me with the warmth of humanity after being inside. Plus those fries were damn good.

I arrived home in time to feed the twelve cats, and as the day rolled to a close, I felt a sense of value in it. Buddhist books were now in a place where no Buddhist books had been. I took a long shower, ate a slice of melted Swiss on rye, lay down on my futon, and glanced over at the Buddha statue on my room altar as I turned out the light.

A few Tuesdays came and went quietly, and then Thanksgiving and late November rolled around. When I walked into the meeting room, a prisoner named Squid asked, "What happened to the books?"

"What do you mean?"

"They're gone," he said.

I was surprised someone was actually looking at them.

"And something isn't right with the cassettes," Squid said. "I went to play 'Zen Mind: Beginners Mind,' but it was just some guy with a guitar singing songs."

"You sure?" I said.

Squid gave me a look; he wasn't the kind of guy who mistook things. A cross between Fonzie and Anthony Hopkins, he was the prison gossip. He knew everything and was always right on the money. I didn't engage with him much, but he was one of the only regulars, and he was always talking. I overheard a lot. Sometimes he predicted fights, and the next week, I'd see some guy show up with stitches.

"Okay, I'll have a look." I stood up, and to my surprise, everyone else did too; the group had taken a stake in the situation. "You guys wait here," I said, but as I left the room, I turned to find them following behind me.

We filed quietly past the Muslim and Christian classes and into the chapel room. The bookshelf was just inside the doorway. We gathered around it. Sure enough, there was a big gap where the Buddhist books had been.

"They must be here somewhere." I searched the bottom and top shelf, and then all the ones between. "Wow," I said, convinced that they were gone. But the talks on tape were still there. I popped one into the chapel's cassette player. The group leaned in around me, and just as Squid had described, a horrible-sounding guitar backed a man belting "Kum Ba Yah."

And with that, I sensed war. The Buddhist group spun and glared through the glass at the Bible school class.

"No big deal," I said, trying to calm them down. "It's just some tapes and free books. We can get more. Let's get back to our talk."

As we walked past the Christian class, James lunged at the glass and gave it a hard, flat-handed spank. Everyone inside jumped as James pointed to the bookshelf. I looked at the woman who taught the class, and her eyes dropped like two guilty rocks. She turned her back to us and kept on with her teaching, but it was too late. Our group flanked me.

"Okay, okay," I said, grabbing the garage-door alarm clipped to my robe. "Let's go back to our room!"

To my surprise, they started back toward our room without a fuss. It was as if I'd told a group of starving children to form an orderly line and to take only one piece of bread each. I realized then that they regarded me as some kind of authority figure, or rather, they needed someone to occupy the top spot in their prison hierarchy in order to function. The human mind always tries to place the ego in "better than or worse than" category relative to everyone else. I closed the door, and we all sat back down. Then the group erupted.

"This is bullshit! They stole from us!" It was the first time I'd seen so much life in the men. Their dead eyes turned fiery, and I was reminded how ugly anger can make people. I sat quietly and let them grouse for a bit. Finally they ran out of gas, and Squid piped up. "How we gonna get more books, Kusala?"

"I think this is a good time to talk about anger," I said. "Think of anger as holding a bunch of hot coals in your hands. It only hurts the person holding the coals. Anger changes the way we think, speak, and act, and that is our karma."

I explained that karma begins with thinking, and thinking creates intentions. The intentions guide our speech and actions, and once our karma is out in the world, there is no getting it back. The result of all that karma is called vipaka, a Buddhist word that means "consequences." So everything we think, say, and do has some kind of consequence, and in Buddhism, we measure the consequences in a personal way: are we suffering more, or suffering less?

Life is the longest, most complex game we're ever going to play, and in Buddhism, the winners suffer less. And ultimately, they don't suffer at all, because a Buddhist uses karma to his or her advantage, fostering intentions rooted in generosity, kindness, and wisdom, not greed, hatred, and anger.

"So how we gonna get more books?" someone from the back repeated.

Nobody cared about my speech on anger.

We came to an agreement that Squid would be the librarian. Instead of storing the books on the bookshelf, he would loan them out from his cell. It was a pretty simple solution compared to all-out war against the Christians.

I went back to the center that afternoon a bit saddened about the woman who taught the Christian class. I decided to give her the benefit of the doubt. She probably didn't have anything to do with the theft of the books. The experience again reminded me that all beings, inside prison and out, suffer from delusions and feelings of separateness. I sent the woman some metta (loving kindness), with a wish that no harm would come to her, and that she would find a way in her religion to peace.

Around the same time, I got a call from my friend Susan in Venice Beach, and she invited me down to meet her friend Jeff Gold, a retired record executive. Jeff had been attending meditation classes at a local center, and she thought we might hit it off. Jeff had been the first employee of Rhino Records and was a significant figure in the music business. After Rhino, he went on to work at A&M Records and then Warner Brothers. All of the bands he worked with were iconic, top tier. He began in artist development and then moved into art direction for albums.

Jeff was also an avid vinyl collector and had scads of rare versions of all the best records. His listening room was like an archival vinyl library.

I hadn't been to Venice in a while, so one morning in 1998 I hopped on Venice Blvd. and went for a visit. I remember he had a beautiful bamboo floor in his home, the first I'd ever seen. Susan had been right about Jeff and me hitting it off. What I hadn't counted on was the impact that meeting Jeff would have on the rest of my life and all the people I would come to know as a result.

"You really should get a computer," Jeff said.

"I'd love to, but they're expensive."

"Susan, you just got one," he said. "How much was it? Like $1,200?"

She nodded.

"Jeff," I said, "that's way beyond the realm of what I can afford."

"Okay, how about this?" he said. "I'll give you the money for the computer, but you have to pay me back. I don't care how long it takes, and there's no interest. I just think it would be a good thing for you to have."

I was a bit uncomfortable with the arrangement, and the cost would be around $1,300 all together, but something told me to take the generous offer. So I did. I ended up paying him back in less than a year, and that computer shifted the whole trajectory of my work and life.

It was a blue, see-through iMac, the first model available with Bondi blue casing, inspired by the clear aqua water of Australia's Bondi Beach. The computer was egg-shaped, one piece, and it took hard discs instead of the old floppy discs. I was excited to learn how to use it, as I found computers and technology fascinating, especially given that I came up in an era when a cordless phone was a big deal.

I told everyone about my recent acquisition, which led to someone giving me a used copy of Dreamweaver 2, which I used to create my first webpage. All it had were the basics, my name and address, but I spent hours and hours learning how to build and connect additional pages.

Then I got a used graphics program from a friend, which allowed me to resize images. It seemed like such a big deal at the time: now I could have my name, address, *and* a photo of the center on my site. I loved designing the pages and shrinking the images to just the right size.

When I saw my work online for the first time, I felt I had made it somehow; it seemed like a big deal. Even these days, I update my online presence a few times a month. The Urban Dharma website ranks high on the Google search list because it's been around so long, and there weren't many Buddhist resources in English online until the mid-2000s. The site now has over two thousand web pages.

I also have a YouTube channel, a Facebook page, and an Apple and Amazon Music podcast. As of July 2023, I average about fifteen thousand downloads a month.

And to think it's all because Jeff Gold offered to finance the computer. It's all connected. You just never know how one thing can mushroom and grow. Maintaining the dharma online is one of the most meaningful aspects of my work as an urban monk. If I had been living in the countryside without technology, I doubt the global reach would have happened.

They say that time passes quickly when one does the same things repetitively. A BBC program purported that this phenomenon has something to do with the way the mind stamps time. If the mind senses a similar behavior or experience over and over, it slows the generation of time-marking memories. Your mind takes a "staycation" of sorts, and if it has collected enough data on the experience, your memory checks in only periodically to see if anything has changed with regard to the "known." Hence the adage, "The days blend together"—not because time actually shifts, but because the mind's perception of time does.

But during my weekly prison visits, unfortunately, my mind never took that staycation. The visits didn't fall into a groove; they never felt fast or familiar, but they never felt slow either. The experience held to its own prison time zone, each visit dipped in a new vein of dissonance, which I tried to shower off as soon as I arrived back at the center.

It was now Christmas time, and cheap holiday trinkets were strewn about the prison. Against the beige of the prison walls, the holiday decorations felt more eerie than festive. Someone had donated two hundred packs of incense to IBMC, so I brought some up to give out to the men. I wasn't sure how incense would go over, but they ended up liking it. I gave the extra packs to Squid to distribute, and he kept them with the books and tapes. The following week, Squid asked for more, and the following week, I brought more. The week after that, he asked for more again.

"That's over a hundred packs of incense," I said. "There's only like twenty men in our group on a good day."

"Yeah…no…yeah, you're right." He stepped in close and lowered his voice. "I can get two cigarettes per pack of stinky stick. Can you get more?"

I shook my head. "That's mighty resourceful of you, but I can't be involved in contraband. I gave you those on good faith, to give out to others, to practice generosity. Not for profit."

"What difference does it really make?"

"Try it and find out."

"It don't work like that, Rev. I'd run out."

"Everything runs out," I said.

His dead eyes looked into mine and then out the window.

"Don't sell the books or tapes or anything else I give you, okay?"

He smirked at my ignorance. If the other stuff had been worth anything, he'd already have sold it.

As I rode home on the bike, I began to think about possessions. I thought about the whole idea of owning stuff and selling stuff; it's all really just a big illusion propagated by receipts. Nothing is really ours to sell, because we don't really own it. If we were actually in control of it, then we could command something never to break or stop working. We're just kind of renting all the stuff we think we own, until it no longer works, or gets lost, or loses it's appeal. The ride home went very fast because I rode fast. The prison work was wearing on me. Just a few more months, I told myself.

When I got back to the center, Princess the cat lay in my room, waiting to die. Mara, the lord of death, had been on his way to her for the last few weeks. A few days earlier, she stopped eating, and on this day, she stopped drinking. Princess lay in the bed I'd made for her inside a UPS box. She seemed calmer in there than when she was on my bed. I think the walls of the box made her feel safe.

She lay with eyes half-closed, and her thin body rocked from side to side, trying to find whatever comfort was left in this life. Sleep had been a refuge, but now that seemed to have been taken from her.

I've struggled with the idea of "natural death" versus "assisted death" for years. Anyone who has watched their animal suffer knows the conundrum. With so many euphemisms like "putting them to sleep," it's easy to overlook the fact that assisted death is an act of killing. But given the first precept I took, which is not to take life, I can't see any way that euthanasia is all right. As the center's caretaker, part of my role was to allow my heart to be broken over and over again as the cats went. After all, they had karma too, and how they passed into death could determine where they went next. So I couldn't bring myself to meddle. And a few of the cats died with surprising ease, without suffering. But Princess wasn't going to be so lucky.

It was a Sunday night, Christmas Eve, and as the time crept closer to midnight, Princess began to call out with little meows every fifteen minutes or so, just to see if I was with her. We had a call and response going on; my voice seemed to comfort her.

As midnight approached, I shut down the computer, closed my book, and said goodnight to her. I was nearly asleep when I heard lots of scratching. When I turned on the light, Princess was lying contorted in a very un-catlike way. Her hind legs pressed stiffly out, and her front claws were hooked into the box, pulling and kneading, pulling and kneading, fighting with the unseen. Princess had begun to die. And she wasn't going to go easily.

"It's okay, Princess," I said lightly, touching the back of her neck. I began to chant, "Om Mani Padme Hum." Twenty minutes passed without change; the only movement was her claws, clinching and latching onto the cardboard, clinching and latching over and over. I sat there useless and in tears. "Leave her alone," I mumbled to Mara. "Let her go in peace, you bastard."

I moved from the chair back to the bed and pulled the box close. The pope was on TV giving the world Christmas Mass from the Vatican. I watched with the sound low so as not to disturb Princess. And right when the Pope was giving the blessing, I looked down into the box and knew that she was gone. I put my hand on her side—total stillness.

As the pope's words rang out in prayer, the room seemed to fill with a different kind of energy, a vacancy that was palpable.

Princess and Mara were gone, another life pulled from this realm and set in motion to another. I cried for a while, not for her death but over the suffering she'd gone through. I made an offering of incense and sent wishes to Princess for a fast and advantageous rebirth. It was all so surreal: the choir singing on TV, the Catholic procession, and Princess's body curled like a fur stole in the box. I lay there most of the night, the box on the bed next to me; I'm not sure why.

In the morning, I buried her. I was reassured to think that she would likely take a human rebirth as a Catholic in her next life. After all, the pope's words were the last thing she heard.

The next week at the prison, I was giving a talk on the avoidance of harsh speech when we heard three gunshots nearby. Everyone froze. Three more shots sounded, and within a half-second, the auto locks engaged, locking every door and sending a cascade of echoes throughout the grounds.

Everyone ran to the window. There were a few men outside seated in the fetal position, knees to chest, arms folded in, in accordance with protocol.

When I turned around, the woman who taught the Christian class was headed for the door to the yard. She yanked at it. The handle spun. She yanked again with a tinge of B-movie horror panic.

The men watched her like prey. I'd often thought about how hard it must be for her, surrounded by sexual predators who hadn't had sex in a long time. Christian or not, their eyes were on her now, more than ever.

I thought about going to her but decided she wouldn't want that, that it might make her seem weak. Also we'd received instructions not to leave our assigned groups in the event of a lockdown. I trusted that there were reasons for the rule. The last thing I wanted was headline that read, "Buddhist Monk Breeches Protocol," followed by a story of injury or death. When you're in robes, you have to think about the results of even the tiniest action, as you're representing something far greater than yourself.

I glanced at the Muslim volunteer in the neighboring room. We made quick eye contact, and he ritualistically transmitted nothing before looking away. Behind him, a few Muslims started to stand and step toward the glass window of their classroom, staring into ours. I looked behind me and saw the same thing happening among the Buddhists. The Christians followed suit, but they were only sport watching. Squid started talking fast in Spanish. Apparently, one of the Muslims had a beef to settle with a man in our group.

I took in the whole situation: three groups of hardened men, one terrified woman, one nonviolent monk, one Muslim teacher, all of us locked under the same roof with nothing but an open doorway and a few panes of glass between. It felt like the chute of a horserace a moment before the bell.

I looked at my guys—somehow they'd become "my guys" in that moment—and I thought, "The Buddhists are faster and leaner and more nimble. They'll kick some ass and protect me."

What? Who was that in my head? My mind was now spouting prison talk. The poison of delusion had seeped in. I remembered the garage door alarm clipped to my robe, but it wouldn't have mattered. The guards were all busy attending to far more serious matters, like quelling a possible riot or removing an angry inmate from the yard.

The room felt suddenly hot as James stepped in with the pack.

"Well," I said, "let's get back to it. Let's all sit down." My tone was unconvincing. Nobody moved but me.

I made my way back to the chairs. It was like walking alone in the forest, very still and very quiet.

"Where were we?" I said, addressing two elderly men who had remained seated.

It was the longest four minutes of my life.

It felt like we were all standing on the corners of a weak little raft, and if one group of men moved, we were all going underwater. The Christian woman stood by the door, hunch-backed, her arms tightly hugging herself. She stared out the window, unwavering; I think she was praying the whole time.

Just when it felt like the raft was about to tip, the sound of a rusty tambourine jangled. A guard had come to unlock the door.

"Okay, everyone back to cell block," he said. The guard stood in the doorway, oblivious to the intensity of the situation. The woman saw her chance and darted outside. None of the men moved.

"I said!" the guard reiterated.

The groups of men peeled apart and slowly moved out the door—first the Buddhists, followed by the Christians, followed by the Muslims.

My escort hadn't arrived, so when the men were gone, I sat in the room, taking in the silence. I was stunned, not at the situation but at how easily my mind had lost what little clarity I'd brought with me that day. I had reverted to old mental habits, letting delusion seep in. I was beginning to understand interconnectedness and impermanence on a different level now, recognizing the potency of one's surroundings. Where you are, and who you're surrounded by, can so easily change what your mind becomes.

I breathed a heavy exhale and looked out the window. The men in the field were still seated for the lockdown; they looked like embryos waiting to be born into the long shadows of the afternoon. The sky was a deep, warming blue. Spring was coming, and so was the close of my service commitment in this hell realm.

The next few months at the prison were riddled with detours. Nothing says spring like a Tuberculosis scare, and the prisoners were in quarantine for forty-eight hours. The following week there was a lockdown, so I drove up and then drove right back again. I had four visits left, and given that attendance vacillated between ten and thirty men, I felt it'd be worthwhile to pass the torch, so I contacted a few monks and dharma teachers. Two from a nearby center were interested.

We all met for coffee, and only then did I realize that no paradigm had developed over the course of my prison visits. They had varied widely in format, depending on the timbre of the men. Some days the men were a barrel of questions, some days none of them could sit still, and some days none of them could even raise their eyes. It was less of a teaching experience than an ice skating experience. I could only tell the prospective teachers what I'd done and encourage them to find their own path with the prisoners.

I also recommended a book authored by a guy who'd pioneered bringing spiritual practice into the prison system. *We're All Doing Time*, by Bo Lozoff, is a great book, steeped in universal appeal. I'd found it very useful and was able to get free copies donated to the inmates. But

I felt a little silly recommending a book as preparation for the new teachers. It was like handing someone an eye surgery manual as their only training before for making the first cut.

After the two teachers cleared background checks and attended the protocol briefing, I made arrangements for them to sit in on my class for three weeks in a row.

Luckily, the classes went well, and the teachers enthusiastically agreed to a yearlong commitment.

On the last day, I taught alone and said nothing to the effect of "goodbye" to the men. There were no bonds made and none broken.

Deacon Sam met me at the security booth and walked me out.

"So, any big plans coming your way?"

"Just a chocolate shake from In-N-Out," I said.

He shook my hand, and as I rode through the gates one final time, the only thing I felt was a little hungry.

It was a rare day at In-N-Out, perfect for sitting outside. The usual dust storm had blown off to somewhere else, and

I took a seat at an outdoor patio table under a red umbrella. I pushed the long straw into the milkshake and felt the warmth of the late afternoon sun on my face.

While I was eating, a burger cook came out the back door and crossed to the rear of the parking lot. He carried his little paper hat in both hands, carefully supporting the bottom. He stepped over the curb and walked into the desert's dirt field just beyond the dumpsters, where he gently set the hat on the ground. As he backed away, he put two fingers to his mouth and chirped out a short whistle.

Within seconds, four or five prairie dog heads poked from their holes.

The cook grabbed a milk crate from behind one of the dumpsters and took a seat, tilting his head with satisfaction as the furry pipsqueaks ate their fill from his makeshift bowl. There was no lead prairie dog selling off food, no fighting, no grudges kept from months before. The little guys just huddled and ate, side by side, without contention.

The cook lit a cigarette, exhaled a slow, graceful stream of smoke, and raised his attention to the mountain range on the edge of the horizon.

The critters ate, the cook smoked, and the monk sucked down an especially good milkshake, all of us interconnected, each happily wrapped in the beauty of the others' contentment.

I arrived back at the center after dark, and as I walked toward the house, a single drop of rain splattered on my head. I stood for a minute, listening to the summer rain gather speed through the trees. Then I made my way to the porch, pulled up my favorite wooden chair, and sat, listening to the night rain fall.

Soon after I finished up at the prison, I was asked to speak at diversity month for a church up north. That's where I met the well-known blues player Walter Trout. I'd closed my talk with some blues harmonica, and he came up afterward to say hello. We hit it off like two kids on the first day of junior high and talked for over a half hour.

"You've gotta come play with me," he said in parting. I was shocked at the offer. He was a Grammy-nominated artist, a blues icon, and his invitation was the last thing I'd thought would come from the talk. Every action sets something in motion, and some are more interesting than others.

He said he'd be playing the Irvine Lake Blues Festival in Orange County and invited me to join him onstage there. Prior to the show, his manager emailed me instructions on where to go and where to park, and when I arrived, I picked up my artist pass at the backstage gate. I found Walter in catering, surrounded by a ton of great food and a lounge setup. The crowd was mostly an inland, working-class crowd, and they *loved* Walter. During his encore, he called me up.

Once I got onstage and got my bearings, I looked out at the sea of people staring up at me and took in the whole scene. I was dressed in monk's robes, the band was dressed in denim and leather, and the audience, well, most of them had beer cans in each hand.

A flash of stage fright punched through me until I realized that nearly everyone in the audience was smiling and cheering me on. Even if they were in various states of altered consciousness, it was one of those surreal moments when you think, "This is so far from what I'd ever imagined for my life!"

After the show, Walter wanted me to go sign autographs with him, so he and I were whisked off in a golf cart to the merch booth. I was given a Sharpie and a chair next to Walter, and people lined up—again, completely surreal.

They wanted me to sign T-shirts and CDs; one woman asked that I sign her shoe. It totally blew my mind. Never in a million years would I have thought I'd find myself in that situation. Walter Trout has remained a friend, and to this day, playing with him is a highlight of living life as Kusala.

Chapter 3
Kids, Fire, and Food Poisoning:
The L.A. Juvenile Hall Years 1996-2000

"Hello?" I said groggily, pinning the phone between my futon and ear. I looked at the clock, 9:45 a.m. The last time I remembered making my way back from throwing up in the bathroom was around 4 a.m., so I guessed the food poisoning had finally passed. Tacos in Korea-Town, no big surprise there. Handling cheese isn't a local specialty.

"I'm looking for Kusala Bhikshu?" a voice through the phone said.

"This is he," I said, rolling over on the futon and looking out the window. It was cloudy, a dark morning.

"This is Noy Russell from the L.A. County Central Juvenile Hall. I saw the article about you a few days ago and was wondering if you might have some time to come talk with our kids?"

When he said "kids," my dehydrated food poisoning brain flashed to the scene of teething kids behind jail bars. "I'm sorry, could you say that again?"

Noy Russell's ratio of kids to staff had dropped from 1:150 to about 1:300 during the budget cuts in the mid 90s. Juvenile Hall was desperate for new approaches, and he'd spearheaded a program that invited spiritual parishioners from diverse traditions to come speak with the kids.

"You interested?" he asked.

I paused, thinking of my experience with the men's prison.

Noy continued, "When it comes down to it, they're just kids. Most are between eleven and eighteen, and a lot of them are in a tremendous amount of pain. I could give you a tour so you can feel it out?"

I thought that was a good idea, so the next day I went. Juvenile Hall was in the civic district on the east side of downtown L.A. It wasn't a good area. In the 1930s, the building had originally been the USC psych ward, and it still felt like it. Institutional oddities were sprinkled throughout, like tile in weird places on the wall, metal window frames with wire over them, a strange color palette of canary yellow and taffy blue. Call buzzers perched on walls, and electrical outlets hung at head level. There were guards, razor wire, and tight security, just like at the men's prison.

Noy Russell was a tall, healthy-looking Black man. He took me around to the gymnasium, the cafeteria, the outdoor commons, and we also walked through the residential housing area.

The boys' wing was medicinally clean, but it reeked of the chaotic energy bred by adolescence. There were a lot of stripped beds, the linens wadded and thrown to the corners of the room. A pillowcase hung halfway out of a stainless steel urinal.

There were no guards, only "staff" who worked either a day shift or a night shift. The latter required them to sleep on site. Although some of the kids were in for serious offenses, the place didn't feel dark and violent like the prison, just scrambled up somehow.

In fact, Central Juvenile Hall was a holding tank where kids waited for arraignment or participated in rehab. Some parents just left their kids in the custody of the state when they were arrested, and those kids stayed until they could be placed in foster care. On most days, the population of Juvenile Hall was around six hundred to eight hundred kids.

A lot of these boys were victims of systemic racism and were there as a result of what I call the "failure lineage." Most of their parents had married young, had children, never got through school, and collected government assistance. Lots of the boys sold drugs, robbed homes, or prostituted themselves just to get by. Eventually, they'd meet a girl, get her pregnant, and pass on the failure lineage to their own children. It was an unfortunate cycle with lots of suffering.

But one of the biggest assets of the program was its base of volunteer professionals. Scads of doctors, attorneys, artists, musicians, and some celebrities served as guest speakers for the kids. Most of these boys were raised in deficient homes and had never even spoken to a person with a college education. So just conversing with a person from a professional community helped more than a few boys. It allowed them to see that they too could find their way out of their socio-economic situation.

A staff worker rounded the corner with a boy of twelve whose hands were cuffed behind his back. "Hello," Noy said to them both with lightness. It was a bit disturbing to see a child in handcuffs.

"The cuffs are only used during transport," Noy said, intuiting my sentiment. "Other than that, we hardly use them, only in extreme cases. We do have some violent offenders in here though—murder, rape, assault, armed robbery, stuff like that. We have them wear the orange suits, not because they are viewed as a threat, but it's a good way to be sure that they get the most attention and help." It was a nice way of saying it. Noy had a warmth about him that I admired.

I agreed to come once a week and so began the next four years of my service at L.A.'s Central Juvenile Hall. Little did I know that I'd be awarded The Good Samaritan Award by the probation department for the volunteer work. It was some of the most meaningful time I've ever spent.

Three days after that initial visit, I found myself standing in the doorway of a classroom of eighteen teenage boys. They chattered away and huddled in groups like kids at any other school, and all but four were clad in orange jumpsuits.

A tall, blonde, librarian-looking teacher strode over to me and introduced herself.

"You know, because we're part of the state, you can't talk about God, right?"

I smiled like I'd done so often when people put God and

Buddhism in the same sentence.

"Yes, Noy Russell and I talked about that. For today, I'm a Buddhist 'history' teacher," I said.

"Buddhist?" she said, with a tinge of something. "I didn't know you were going to be Buddhist."

"Neither did I."

I think her eyes smiled, but it was hard to tell under her frown. "Just don't talk about God," she repeated and strode back to her desk, leaving me to introduce myself.

I walked to the center of the room and took a breath. The boys were deeply entrenched in kid dynamics. They were punching each other, horsing around, tearing up pieces of paper. A few sat on their desks; one kid stood off by the bookshelf alone.

"Hi, everyone," I said. The boy by the bookcase was the only one who turned to face me. I looked at the teacher, who was busy penciling something into a grade book.

"Hi, everyone," I said again, louder. No one responded.

I pulled the guitar I'd brought from its case. The kid by the bookcase lost interest, jammed a pencil into a sharpener, and began to crank shavings to the ground like parmesan cheese.

I hit one loud G chord on the guitar, and the whole of the room focused like a laser. Then

I played a simple chord progression and started talking over it in a storytelling kind of way. "I see we have a lot in common," I said over the strumming. "We all have the same haircut."

One kid smiled and rubbed his shaven head. I kept

playing and started singing one of the most Buddhist rock songs of all time.

"The Stones!" a kid yelled from the back.

I nodded, and when I came to the first chorus, four or five of them started singing with me.

"You can't, always get, what you want."

It was the perfect segue way into talking about suffering and the story of the Buddha. Fortunately, the Buddhist story is a good fit for any audience; it's got wealth, women, sickness, child abandonment, starvation, death, and a pretty big character arc, to say the least.

I ran down the four noble truths, the eight fold path, and the story of the Buddha, and then I opened the floor for questions. A bunch of hands went up.

"My mom said your religion is the occult. Are you?"

The teacher finally look up from her grade book.

"To some we are, but it's all relative," I said.

"Buddhism is different from most religions; it's one of the few that puts you into the driver's seat. The Buddha was only a teacher, not a god. Buddhism suggests that the answers are within all beings. It's only a matter of getting rid of all the stuff blocking us from seeing those answers." I could tell I was losing them. "It's a do-it-yourselfer philosophy," I said, as they seemed to perk up. This was something they could related to.

Most of these kids were not only responsible for their own well-being at an early age, but circumstances often forced them into acting as parents for their siblings.

"Can anyone tell me what suffering is?" I asked.

Silence.

"Suffering is wanting things to be different than the way they are," I said.

A stillness blanketed the room. "Are there any questions about the Buddha?"

A boy of about fourteen slightly raised his hand. "Why did the prince leave his family?"

"That's a very good question. Who of you here have a baby brother or sister?"

All but one boy raised his hand, and then it hit me. "Now, who of you have a baby son or daughter of your own?"

Six of the eighteen kids raised their hands. Most of them were around fifteen.

"When you spend time with your son or daughter, how much do they require from you?"

A kid said, "Babies need stuff all the time—food, diapers, toys."

"Exactly! The Buddha left his family after his first child was born because he knew he'd never be able to give his full attention to finding a way out of suffering if he was responsible for a child. A child's needs are too great; the commitment would have kept him from his path."

I wrapped up the first class after ninety minutes. The kids were bummed to see me go, but only because math class was next.

"Let's thank Rev. Kusala for spending his time with us today," said the teacher.

A sedated "thank you" mumbled out from the bunch as they pulled out their math books.

I was due to return in a week, and as I walked back to

my motorcycle, I realized these kids were in a place where their lives could shift entirely with just a small turn, the right encouragement, an effective role model. I was grateful to be available to help in such a place.

When I showed up the following week, the only thing that was the same were the orange jumpsuits. Throughout my time working at Juvenile Hall, it was usually different kids each week. I ended up doing most of the talks inside the housing pods, in the multi-purpose room. It felt less formal than a classroom with a teacher; it was just me, the staff, and the boys. We all spoke more freely in this setting.

On my next trip, I brought a group of women dharma teachers who wanted to get involved. This was the only time I gave a talk in the girls' ward, which was as far away from the boys' side as possible.

Compared to the boys' ward, the girls' ward was like a resort—not because the space was different, but because the girls had created more of a home. Cutout magazine pictures hung on the walls; colored pillows were propped on neatly made beds; perfume lined the backs of toilets; and small knick-knacks lay scattered throughout the dorm. Makeup was traded like currency, and so was nail polish, especially black.

I was told that very few of the girls masterminded the crimes they were convicted of; most were in for accomplice charges, a product of being in the wrong place at the wrong time. Absentee parents were the norm, and almost all of the girls were minorities, raised in L.A.'s inner city. Some were products of gang environments; others had never been to a dentist. Many of them read at a grade school level or not at all.

Aside from the foul language, tattoos, and self-made half shirts, the girls looked and acted like any other teenage girls. I saw only three orange jumpsuits on the entire ward. During my talk, I made sure to emphasize that the Buddha said women have the same opportunity for enlightenment as men; he even ordained his stepmother.

As I gave my talk, the incarcerated girls sat quietly, some braiding each other's hair; most listened and even smiled. It was night and day compared to the boys' side, and afterward, several of them lined up to thank me.

After it was all over, a staff member stopped by to give me a note from Noy: "Hi Rev. Kusala. If you have the time, go see Peter Smith in the infirmary, he could use a little boost. If not, no biggie. Thanks for all your help – Noy."

The other dharma teachers were still there, along with one remaining distraught girl. We were all waiting for an escort. I could sense that tears were ready to pop from her eyes as she sat in the corner, her sewing machine leg bobbing up and down.

She was fifteen years old and facing eighteen years in prison. She'd been in her boyfriend's car when a kid in the backseat pulled out a gun and shot a rival gang member who was eating an ice cream cone on a bus stop bench. She and her boyfriend had nothing to do with it, and the boyfriend was so startled that he gunned through a red light. An oncoming car sideswiped them, leaving her boyfriend unconscious, just feet from the scene. She stayed with him while the other kids ran.

At thirteen, she had the experience of watching a gunshot drain the life from a young boy; the medics pronounced him DOA. Her story was reported in the *L.A. Times*.

Madeline, we'll call her, was waiting for an escort to the infirmary. She was due to have the crudely drawn snake tattoo on her throat removed. Juvenile Hall had a pool of volunteer doctors who gave their time to do that sort of work, so when the kids went before the judge, they'd have a clean appearance.

"It's gonna hurt like hell," she said, trying to choke back tears.

"I'll walk over with you," I said. "I have to stop by the infirmiry anyhow."

I said goodbye to the other Dharma teachers and asked Madeline's attendant if I could walk with them. She nodded, and I pulled up a chair next to Madeline. She looked suspicious.

"It's gonna kill," she said again, grabbing at her throat.

She was probably right.

"It can't hurt as bad as it did getting it," I said.

"I don't remember getting it. I was four. My dad was a tattoo artist."

My heart shifted sad in my chest.

"It's a well-equipped hospital ward," I said. "I'm sure they'll give you lots of anesthetics. Maybe you won't even feel it."

"Till it wears off," she said.

"You look like you've lived through worse," I said, fumbling. "I mean, you look like you can hold your own."

She liked that and nodded, but I still felt bad. You always try to say the right thing, but sometimes you don't.

Another girls was passing by the multi-purpose room. She stopped and stared at Madeline with crossed arms.

"Hey, Sissy!" she yelled. "This mascara sucks. It's like two years old." She hurled the tube at us, pegging Madeline in the knee. "I want my money back!"

"Hey!" yelled the attendant. "Marissa, enough!"

Marissa was escorted out of the room.

Madeline's tears were in full sprint down her cheeks.

"It's good you didn't respond," I said.

She wiped her eyes with her sleeve.

"You know, nonviolence is one of the highest skill levels in Buddhism," I said. "Seems like you've got a handle on it."

She raised her head and made eye contact with me for the first time. "What if someone's trying to kill you?"

I'd never been in that situation, but at fifteen, I bet she had. It was the way she said it. Sadness flashed through me.

"Well, if your life is threatened, and there is no other possible way to survive unless you inflict harm, then it's okay. But even then, you'd try to use the least amount of force necessary."

"What the fuck?" she said. "You Gandhi or something?"

I laughed. She did too. For a moment she looked like the teenager she actually was.

"Madeline, maybe just look at today as if you're getting a free makeover. Like you'll get to be a blank slate again. People may even treat you differently without that on your neck. You'll finally be free from a decision that someone else made for you."

"Whatever, Gandhi," she said, but I could see the wheels turning in her head.

"Okay, Maddie," said the attendant, "let's go."

We all walked to the infirmary without saying a word. I couldn't think of a thing to say. She was obviously nervous, and once we got to the front desk of the medical wing, we parted ways like two people on a city bus; she just gave me a nod and kept walking. Apathy was a sad skill most of the kids had seemed to perfect. I watched her posture become more guarded as she proceeded down the hall. With her back to me, she called, "Thanks Gandhi!" and kept walking.

"Enjoy the freedom," I said.

With its tiled walls and wide, institutional hallways, the infirmary reminded me of *One Flew Over the Cuckoo's Nest*, only without Nurse Ratched. I turned to the nurse's desk. A woman sat perched staring at me. She gave my robes the once over and pounded a staple through a packet of papers.

"What can I help you with?"

"Noy Russell asked me to visit a boy named Recci Smith."

Her look softened in the smallest possible increment.

She eyed my robes again, opened her mouth to speak, and decided against it. Instead, she pushed back from the desk and walked me down the long hallways. Almost every bed in the facility was full, girls on one side of the hallway, boys on the other. Later I learned that most of them weren't sick but were under medical supervision for substance abuse detox. As we passed one room, I heard someone throwing up.

Finally we stopped at a closed door.

"This is his room." She put her ear to the door and then unlocked it.

"Hi, Recci," she said. "You have a visitor."

From the doorway, what I saw was eerie. It was like I'd stepped off the set of *ER* and onto Nickelodeon. The room was wallpapered in crayon drawings, and a wizard puppet stuck out from under a kid-sized plastic table.

It felt more like a nursery than a hospital room.

Recci wore a key-lime polo shirt and cargo pants and sat half inside a cupboard below the sink. A pile of small green plastic soldiers lay around his feet. He held one in each hand; they were talking. The nurse took a few steps toward him and squatted. "Recci?"

He ignored her.

"Recci, you have a visitor, this is…" She looked to me.

"Kusala," I said. Something about my voice lifted Recci out of his game; he looked at me, giving me the once over.

"Why are you wearing a dress?" he asked.

"This is Kusala," she said. "He's come to say hello."

Recci looked back down at the pile of soldiers at his feet.

She stood and turned to me. "Just push the buzzer if you need anything," she said, pointing to a switch. "Maggie will be coming in to supervise in a minute."

I nodded, and she left.

Time downshifted; the moment was surreal. Down the hall, teenagers were puking their guts out, coming off drugs, and here was Recci in his key-lime polo shirt, playing the most rudimentary of childhood games. War.

"Why are you wearing a dress?" he asked again.

"It's not a dress," I said. "They're robes."

"Like bathrobes?"

"A little," I said.

"You can be a dead guy," he said, pointing to a pile of soldiers.

"Okay, but what do dead guys do?"

"They scream a lot."

"I don't think they're dead if they're making noise."

"They do. They scream until their mouths die."

I sat down on the floor and pulled a toy soldier from the pile.

"That one is not dead," Recci said.

I put it back. He reached over and selected one for me. "That one's dead."

I stood the soldier upright and started helping the other dead ones up.

"What are you doing? Those are dead." He was growing annoyed.

"This dead one is helping the other dead one," I said.

Recci slid himself from the cupboard and stood. He was about as tall as I was sitting.

"Are you a judge?"

"No," I said.

"Are you here to watch me?"

"No."

"Close your eyes then."

I did. "I'm not here to watch you."

"Are you friends with my dad?" he asked.

"No, I don't know your parents." I opened my eyes.

"You're a stranger?"

"Yep, but since the nurse introduced us, we're not strangers anymore. My name is Kusala."

I wondered where Maggie was. I went over and propped open the door to the hallway. It's never good to be left alone with a child.

Recci looked at the open door.

For lack of anything else to say, I told him that my name meant "skillful."

"What's skillful?"

"In the case of my name, it means causing less suffering."

Recci stood up, went over to the chalkboard, and started teaching a row of stuffed animals the alphabet. It was obvious he spent a lot of time alone.

"You can come to sit here," he said, pointing to the plastic kiddie chair.

I sat down, knees up around my chin.

Recci resumed teaching the animals the alphabet, and when he got to *c*, his lecture eroded into a plea for candy.

"I'm not allowed to bring candy in here," I said.

"Where's my mom?" he asked.

"I don't know."

"Is she coming back?"

"I've never met your mom," I said.

"My mom is gone," Recci mumbled.

I had no idea what to say.

"My mom is gone," he said again.

"What grade are you in?" I asked.

"First."

"What do you do in first grade?"

"In science, it's about dinosaurs."

"I like science. I won first place at the science fair when I was in fourth grade."

"You were in fourth grade?"

"Yes, a long time ago."

"You won first?" he asked.

"Actually I tied for first."

"How can there be two firsts?"

"I don't know. Maybe they trade off the Wednesdays." I was growing a little tired.

Recci grabbed a dirty-looking stuffed rabbit. I wondered what was going on with his mom but knew not to ask.
The staff was conscientious about withholding the kids' circumstances because of the legal ramifications. This allowed me to serve more neutrally, without the distraction of subjective backstories. I was one of the few adults at Juvenile Hall who wasn't there to conduct evaluations or sentencing check-ups. I had nothing to do with the kids' futures, only something to do with their day. It was sort of like how the ice cream man pulls up and does his deal, but never knows what goes on behind the neighborhood doors. I was just there to hopefully offer a few moments of kindness.

But when I looked at this innocent six-year old child, it was hard not to be curious about why he was there.

Recci put a stuffed monkey under his shirt and started

talking to it down his front collar. Eventually he seemed to remember that I was in the room.

"Do you like peanut butter squares?" he asked.

"Yes," I said.

"Make me one."

"I can't do that sort of thing without the nurse's permission," I said.

He threw the monkey against the wall.

"I want peanut butter," he said louder.

My legs were falling asleep in that tiny chair, so I stood and moved toward the door with the agility of an armadillo.

"Don't go!" he screamed.

I froze, not wanting to scare him.

"I'm not leaving yet," I said calmly.

"Why do you wear that dress?" he asked.

"It's my uniform for work."

"What work?"

"I go around and help people who are not feeling well."

"Sick?"

"Some are sick, but I also talk with people who are feeling sad or mad."

"Do you have a blue dress too?"

"No, just brown, just this one."

"Brown like a toad."

I laughed. "Or brown like a bear.

When the nurse comes back, I can ask her about the peanut butter." I walked to the wall of drawings. "What do you like to draw?"

"I like red," he said, pulling the chair to the table.

"Paper, please." He pointed to the crayons and a pad of paper high out of reach on the cabinet. I took it down and gave it to him.

He began to draw and then slipped a purple crayon into his mouth, snapped off the end, and started chewing, swallowing it like licorice.

"Stop!" I said, pulling the crayon out of his hand. I thought of choking, a forever-bluish tooth, poison control.

"I do it all the time," he said. "I'm hungry."

I believed him. I pushed the button, and the nurse soon appeared. I told her about the crayon.

"Peanut butter?" Recci said.

She walked to the cabinet and took out a sandwich sealed in a Ziploc. "I was going to give it to him later, but if he's hungry now..."

"Yes!"

Recci was happy. He shared a bite with his dirty stuffed monkey.

"Okay," she said as he settled into a chair. She switched on the TV, which was the cue for my exit. I waved goodbye, and the nurse followed, closing his door behind us.

"He likes you," she said as we walked. "He doesn't get to talk with many men."

"Glad I could help." I said. "How long has Recci been in here?"

She sighed and came out with it all.

"This time, about two weeks. He burned down his house," she whispered. "Twice."

My first thought was: who leaves matches around for

kids—twice?

"He doesn't get much contact with men or really anyone but nurses. We have to keep him out of the population. It's not good to have a six-year-old with the older kids. A few years back, his mom got a ton of money from a court settlement, and she basically became a stay-at-home drunk. She almost burned alive in the last fire. She was passed out in bed when it started. So she's terrified to have him around. She's made it clear that she wants the state to take him; it's a loss across the board for everyone. I mean, she's a horrible mom, but on the other hand, he has burned down the house two times in two years. And his dad is gone."

All I could do was shake my head.

"The sad thing is, he's been evaluated by a million people, and every report just comes back saying he's starved for attention, not fire obsessed."

"What'll happen to him?" I asked.

She was quiet. I couldn't tell if she was emotional or thinking.

"You should come back and talk with him if you can," she said. "It's good for him to be with a male."

As I walked down the maze of hallways toward the exit, I began to doubt my usefulness. What good had it done for me to see him? I wanted to give Recci something that would help, but all I could do was show up, and I wasn't convinced that was good enough. Undoubtedly, there would be some effect—karma tells us that. I decided to hang my hat on that.

It was important that I not get emotionally involved

with the kids. If I did, I'd be doing us both a disservice; I'd burn out from compassion fatigue.

For the next two months, Recci and I ate peanut butter sandwiches, played war, and eventually got the little green soldiers into peace talks. When the conflict ended, some of them were hired on by the U.N. as international peacekeepers, but most of them returned to their families.

Then one day when I arrived, the nurse said, "Recci's not here anymore, he was transferred."

"Oh." I stalled in disbelief. I almost asked when he was coming back, but I could tell by the way she'd said it that the move was permanent. "Okay then," I said, letting him go.

"You were really nice to come so much," she said. "He liked you."

As I turned onto New Hampshire Ave ,I hit the brakes hard. My heart sank. I got off the motorcycle and surveyed the pavement. There on the ground was Misty the cat. Her black and white fur was matted with red. Damn cars.

Misty had been at the center for about seven years, and seeing her body like that was horrible. I crouched; a few tears polka dotted the cement. After parking my bike, I went to the backyard gardening shed, looking for a box. All I could find was a scrap of plywood and an old towel. I grabbed gardening gloves too.

Her body was a little warm as I rolled her into the towel.

"What happened!" screeched Carl from his window two doors down. I could hear him running full tilt down the stairs. I waited for the slap of the screen door as he burst out in a full run toward me.

"It's Misty," I said, folding the towel over her.

"What? Misty Misty Misty," he said in an obnoxious sing-song. "Misty Mist—"

"Stop that!" I said.

Carl was unfazed. "Misty, Misty . . ."

"She's dead," I said, and Carl stopped on a dime. He'd tuned into my grief.

"She's dead," he repeated.

Carl slid the scrap of plywood closer to the towel, I rolled her onto it, and we started toward the zendo.

Carl walked behind me as I carried the makeshift stretcher, and then he ran ahead to hold the door open.

"Why don't you come in and help me bless Misty?" I said, but the door was closing behind me, and Carl was already gone.

Carl had never stepped foot in the zendo, There was something about it that he didn't like, or was afraid of. Whenever I asked him about it, all he said was "I'll break it," but refused to explain further. Somehow the zendo was Carl's kryptonite. On occasion, when I'd had a bad day, and he was really annoying, I'd capitalize on his aversion to the zendo, using it to escape from him.

I looked down at the towel and then up at the Buddha, who sat brightly lit at the far side of the room. At times, the zendo felt like a tired place filled with old relics that looked almost prop-like. But that day, it was the complete opposite. Every statue and picture, every flower on the altar felt alive, giving its fullest.

I laid Misty on the ground in front of the Buddha and lit

some incense. I opened the towel a little, letting the smoke waft onto her fur. I sat and did a few chants, sending wishes for a fast and good rebirth into an upper realm.

I don't know how long I was there, but when I came out of meditation, the incense had burned to a nub, and the mound of towel sitting on the scrap wood plank looked more like a fancy bread basket at an Italian restaurant.

Misty felt gone. I bowed to the Buddha, brought her body to the backyard, and set her next to the shed. I got a shovel.

As I dug, the ground didn't lift easily. I thought of Madeline from Juvenile Hall, sleeping her first night with a clean neck, and all the death that occurred on the planet that day. It was dark, and the digging brought the colony of cats over. I could see their nighttime eyes watching, shining electric as they peered from hiding spots around the yard. I gathered some flowers from a shedding bougainvillea vine and sprinkled them into the grave on top of Misty. I filled in the dirt and went inside—time to open the zendo for meditation.

The next morning it was raining, and by the day's end, the moisture had all but erased the freshness of Misty's grave. When the sun peeked through around sunset, casting a quick light before dusk, it was as if Misty had never been. The cats would not miss her, and the ground would absorb her body, making food for other beings. There were no grieving descendants, no words said on her behalf. Misty had lived, eaten, walked around a lot, and then died without leaving much of a trace. If only humans possessed the same capacity for such grace.

The next day a woman called and asked if I would come

volunteer at Camp Kilpatrick, the juvenile probation camp in Malibu where many kids from Juvenile Hall transferred after a trial mandate.

As one thing always leads to another, I found myself accepting the invitation. "See you Friday," I said after taking down the info.

The camp was off Point Dune Road, and while the Malibu area is known for celebrities and wealth, these boys were from a different world. The camp's location, at the base of some beautiful hill, was chosen to provide urban kids exposure to a rural environment, the hope being that the setting would shift their consciousness and life paths.

Most of the boys were mandated to serve their time while receiving substance abuse counseling, emotional management, schooling, and job skills. Athletics were emphasized to promote group dynamics and team building. Camp Kilpatrick had a low staff-to-student ratio, and the program provided tutoring and access to mentors.

As I rode through the camp gates, it looked like part school and part camp. A woman who had studied Tibetan Buddhism ran the place and greeted me. The camp was part of the probation department in L.A. County. The woman was part of Thubten Dhargye Ling, a center in Long Beach.

"Find it okay?" she asked.

"Yes, what a beautiful ride. These roads are built for motorcycles."

As she showed me around, the place felt very different

from Juvenile Hall. The boys were a bit rowdy but somehow more accessible. Their toughness was still evident, but there was also the innocence of youth.

I saw a fourteen-year-old boy making his bunk bed with care; another folded socks on his bed. It was chore time, and it felt like there wasn't an attitude of resistance, though one boy sat atop his bunk and pretended to smoke a paper cigarette.

He gave me a look that said, "Who the hell is this guy?"

Outside, a group of boys was sitting in the common area listening to a man talk about being an actor.

"We have a lot of guest speakers," she said. "It's part of the program. We expose the kids to people who can speak to a different way of life. Lots of actors, attorneys, doctors, and comedians come and talk about how they got where they are, and sometimes they even offer to help start the kids in training, or school. When I heard you play the harmonica downtown at the beginning of your talk, I immediately knew you'd be great up here. We've been trying to start a music class for two years, and unfortunately, most of the musicians I've contacted come a few times but then can't come again."

I stalled. "I'm not a formally trained musician," I said. "I really wouldn't know how to teach someone harp."

"Well, they're not formally trained music students either, so they won't know the difference," she said. "Anyway, could you possibly find a way to get some harmonicas here?"

"I'll think about it."

I can't remember how I met Venice Beach Susan, but

she ended up accompanying me to the camp quite often

Her passion was environmental issues, and she spoke about them to the kids. Susan was also the person who introduced me to Jeff Gold, my music industry friend who gave me the loan for my first computer.

Jeff was happy to help and knew John Popper, frontman and harp player for Blues Traveler. Jeff spoke to John, and a few days later, a large box of Hohner harmonicas landed on my doorstep.

At Camp Kilpatrick, we held the music lessons in a formal classroom. The kids sat at desks, and there was a good chalkboard. On that day, about fifteen boys speckled the chairs in front of me. The football team practiced simultaneously, and many of the kids who landed with me had discipline problems and had lost their sporting privileges.

"If the Buddha had been a musician," I said, "I think he'd have played the blues. Blues music seems to capture the essence of the First Noble Truth: life is filled with suffering."

I put the box of harmonicas on the top of a desk at the front of the room.

"There's enough for all of you," I said, opening the box.

It was as if I'd fired a starting gun; they jumped up and ran to the box.

The first kid who got one blew it loudly. "Are these broken?" he asked.

"Nope. They're brand new, and you can keep 'em. Just bring 'em to class next time."

I imagined a boy coming home from Camp Kilpatrick

holding up a shiny harmonica to his mom and saying, "Look what I got at camp." How might parents respond?

Because the L.A. school system had cut much of the budget for art and music, these kids didn't get exposure to musical instruction. It was ironic that they could get exposure to music only if they were locked up. I knew the impact music could have, and the focus it demands in terms of listening. I knew it would help them think differently, think without words, think with sound.

There were enough harmonicas for all the kids and a few left over. I watched them blow in experimentation and listened to the air become wonderfully jagged and cluttered with odd notes.

I decided to start simply.

"Okay, so let's make a chord. I want you to cover two holes with your mouth and blow," I said, breathing out a simple tone. It took a while for the kids to find it.

"What note is that?" asked a boy.

"It's the one we're all playing," I said. "I'm not sure what its proper name is, but we've all found it."

I looked at the staff member, who looked away. I was a music teacher who knew nothing about notes.

"It's a fuckin' F," a kid said, blowing hard.

The staff attendant didn't move a muscle. I often was impressed by how they managed certain situations; they were wise at picking their battles.

"Why do you play the harmonica?" a boy asked.

"I play the harmonica because it's fun."

"Oh, it's not that fun." He was being a downer. There

always seemed to be one.

"It's meditative," I said, "and speaking of meditation, for the last half hour we've been listening to the sound of harmonicas; now let's listen to some silence."

I closed with a few minutes of meditation with the kids, which was like trying to walk a flock of birds into a box. But after we were done, there was a palpable shift; for a moment they seemed to have landed on an iota of quiet. Most of them left the classroom like a marching band, blowing on the harps. I knew I'd have to find someone who knew about music to help me.

I racked my brain and finally called my friend Denise Kaufman. She was an adept surfer, a well-known yoga instructor in celebrity circles, and she also played bass and harmonica in a band called The Ace of Cups. I thought she might want to help, but she was at her other home in Hawaii and would be there for an extended period of time.

A few days later, I received a random email from John G. McDuffie, a professional guitar player in L.A. He'd heard me speak and wanted to come along to help. It was one of those moments when a crack in the universe opens and invites you to stare in. Kismet. John was exactly the person I needed at just the right time. Who knows how that stuff works, but it's hard to look away when it does.

John had played on many people's records and had done a lot of touring. For many years, he'd been Rita Coolidge's music director. He was a skilled pedal steel and dobro player too, formally trained. John was the missing link for the music program; he could teach it. He and I hit it off quickly, and we arrived at the next class together. I started with a short talk on suffering.

"Doesn't life suck?" I began.

All the boys sat motionless, staring at me, questioning.

"It sucks, right?" I repeated. "You look around, and all you see are poor people struggling, sick people dying from disease and addiction, people killing one another, our family members dying, and some of us aren't even allowed to play football."

"Yeah, our lives suck in here!" a kid yelled, louder than necessary.

"I bet it does, but you know what? Life sucks out there too, and that's why life sucks in here." These kids were suffering, and for me to tell them that life wasn't rainbows and supermodels—well, I had their attention. It was the perfect segue into teaching them to write blues lyrics. I looked over at John, who'd been sitting at a corner desk with his guitar across his lap.

"So we've got about twenty minutes left," I said, "and we're doing music for the rest." I was surprised at the excitement they showed whipping out their harmonicas and blowing. I introduced John, he and I played a blues song together, and then he took over teaching timing, notes, and blues theory. I learned along with the kids.

The day closed with everyone playing a blues scale in unison. It was meaningful to see them looking like kids again as they peered over the tops of their harmonicas at us, blowing out notes. For the moment, I'm pretty sure they weren't worrying about drugs, violence, or poverty. They were present; past and future were suspended; the music was the only reality.

"We'll have you write blues lyrics next time," I said in closing.

People think that being a monk is a relaxing and quiet way to live. They imagine that most of our time is spent in silence, deep in reflection, and the rest of the day is reading scripture. While there is much of that at the beginning of monastic life, things change after a monk receives training and ordination and takes his vows; the main concern becomes helping beings to suffer less. And once you help one person, it starts a pipeline that eventually widens and spreads. Often times the people you help are more willing to help others and so on.

My average week involves responding to prayer requests, visiting the sick, giving dharma talks, leading group meditations, officiating memorial services and weddings, and giving informational presentations. Over the years, working the press has been an on-and-off responsibility too. I've been contacted by outlets such as *The Los Angeles Times*, History Channel, PBS, radio programs, and other media to give the "Buddhist" view on various topics. Often, there is little time for my own meditation practice outside of leading the center's program, and even less time to read or sleep. A lot of monks are so busy that they don't get more than six hours a night. So "chop wood, carry water" couldn't be further from one's life when living at a center situated in Los Angeles.

For twenty years, one of my duties at the center has

been to facilitate the Wednesday, Friday, and Sunday nights meditations from 7:30 to 9 p.m. I open the doors, burn the incense, welcome newcomers and long-timers, and keep track of the time during the sits. Afterward, we all talk a bit, and sometimes people pull me aside to discuss an issue they are having. This part of my service has been one of the most rewarding aspects of being a monk, and also one of the most annoying.

But some nights are just plain interesting. Like when two newcomers—let's call them Dan and Jan—showed up for meditation. Normally the group size ranged between one and fifteen people, and that night, there were seven. Anthony was a semi-successful actor/director who'd gained a cult following for his series that starred a demon-possessed cat. Anthony's girlfriend seemed totally normal except that she was dating Anthony. Marcus was a regular who already sat meditating at the beginning of the session. And then there was Rebecca, an awkward, tall, forty-something who always wore the same clothes and looked homeless, though I got the impression she had money.

Jan and Dan arrived in vastly different attire. He was in loose jeans and a collared shirt, and she was in black leather pants, platform heels, and a chain-link fence of jewelry around her neck.

They moved toward the cushions on the floor, where Dan took a seat and curled into a cross-legged pose. Jan remained standing, staring down at the cushion as if it were a toilet in a New York City subway station. After an awkward pause, she slipped two fingers into her belt loops, hiked her pants up, and tried to sit. The pants squeaked as she came to a squat, and she sort of tipped onto the cushion butt first. To my relief, she landed rather gracefully. Then she grasped her ankles and wrenched them in, somehow forming a perfect cross-legged position. She smiled the saddest little smile at Dan as she took shallow breaths.

"If you want to stack a few cushions," I said, rising to grab an extra, "it might be more comfortable."

"No, no, I'm fine," she insisted.

I sat back down and struck the singing bowl, which signaled the start of our first twenty minute sitting. The practice at IBMC consists of three meditation periods with three-to-four-minute breaks in between. We all settled in for the first sitting rather well, except for Jan.

You could hear her start to squirm, the hundred pounds of jewelry jangling.

I didn't open my eyes and surmised from the sound of things that she stood up, readjusted, and sat back down to give it another shot. More minutes passed with more of the same. Her bracelets chimed as she scratched and itched, and her pants squeaked with the transference of weight; the longer she sat, the more she moved.

Finally Jan grabbed her shoes and walked out the door. Dan followed. Once they were out on the porch, they were under the misconception that we couldn't hear them.

"Are you okay?" Dan asked.

"I've never done this so . . . formally," she said.

"You've never done this? But you said you had."

"Well, I have, like in yoga class, on my back for two

minutes. I thought we'd be in chairs, and there would be music. I thought the guy would at least say something."

Dan exhaled. "What do you wanna do?"

"I don't know," she said with an *I wanna get the hell out of here* tone.

"Is it bad if we leave?"

"I feel a little bit bad about leaving in the middle; it's distracting for everyone."

Apparently, talking loudly outside the door wasn't. There was a long pause.

"Just let me get my shoes," Dan said.

We heard car keys jangling, and Jan's high heels clicked down the porch steps and out into the street. The zendo door creaked back open, and Dan snuck in quietly and sat, putting on his shoes. The first twenty minutes were up, so I rang the gong. Dan apologized, and I invited him to come back. The group took a short break, and about thirty seconds into the second meditation, the zendo door creaked open again, and Dan resumed his seat on the cushion, where he remained for the rest of the night. When the final bell rang, we all stayed seated as the elephant in the room swayed.

"She took my car," Dan said softly.

We were all quiet.

"I can't believe she took my car."

He didn't seem mad, just dumbfounded.

"Well," I said, "I guess you guys have a little to talk about later."

"This was our first date."

"No way," said Anthony.

"Well, the first time we met in person, anyway. We got a coffee before we got here. That's probably where she took my car."

"You brought her here on a first date?" Anthony said.

Rebecca got up and walked toward the bathroom. "Cheap date," she said.

"She was the one who wanted it!" he said. "I found you guys in the online. It sounded like a good idea."

The group's resounding silence suggested that it was anything but a good idea, and was further punctuated by Rebecca flushing the toilet in the next room.

"I don't even know if she ever did this before," Dan said.

"Kusala," Anthony said, "what do you usually tell first-timers?"

"I do the same thing now as I did on my first day at the center," I said. "I experience the breath. The rest happens naturally if you sit with the breath enough times. The breath is essential."

"Essential for what?" Anthony asked.

"For life," I said. "If you're not breathing, you don't have to meditate. The breath is the ultimate beginning and end of our existence. It's always with us—at least you hope so, or you've got some pretty big problems that meditation isn't going to fix. If you focus enough, you can even forget you're wearing leather pants."

"Does anyone live in Hancock Park?" Dan asked.

Marcus gave him a ride. It was the perfect ending to a

rather confusing day.

After that, Dan started coming regularly. And we found out that Jan had run into Carl on the lawn that night while she was waiting for Dan to get his shoes. Carl was enthralled with Jan's leather pants, so in an effort to get away, she'd driven around the block and had gotten pulled over for an illegal turn. She hadn't tried to take Dan's car after all, and they ended up dating for over a year. You might assume you know the story, but the reality isn't always what we think.

The following week, John and I were back at Camp Kilpatrick. We taught the boys the quintessential blues riff "I'm a Man," by Muddy Waters. We structured it like the old chain gangs did, call and response. Each boy would sing his lyrics, and the class would echo them. Not surprisingly, they had a ton of suffering to sing about: welfare troubles, deadbeat dads, drunken moms, car crashes. F-bombs flew, it all came out, and the kids loved it.

John and I left the camp feeling it was time well spent. We also got accolades from the staff, who said that during the week, some of the kids would collect outside and take turns freestyling blues lyrics.

The Camp Kilpatrick "music program" later led to my being asked to appear on a nighttime TV talk show called *Vibe*, hosted by Sinbad. When the show producer called, she explained that they usually sent a limousine to pick up guests, but they wanted me to ride my motorcycle so that they could film it for the opening segment. To be honest, I was a bit disappointed; I'd never been in a limo. But she was right: arriving on the motorcycle in my robes was a cinematic entrance.

After I did an on-set interview with Sinbad, talking about teaching music at Camp Kilpatrick, the segment ended with me performing a blues song on my harp with Sinbad's house band. It was another one of those "how did I get here?" moments. What had begun with me fumbling around, trying to teach music to a room full of jailed teens, ended with me playing harmonica on national TV with an all-star band.

I couldn't believe how much energy I got from the experience. The lights, the band, the audience—I can see why people get hooked on show business.

The funny thing was, even though it all seemed impromptu on TV, it wasn't—nothing ever really is in Hollywood. Earlier in the day, I'd come in to rehearse the song with the band and do a sound check. I remember wanting to be like Sonny Terry and chose to play in the key of A, because that's the one he liked. It takes more air because it's a lower key, and I recall being winded after the show, wishing I'd chosen the straightforward key of C. To further complicate things, I was on the mic at the sound check, but during the performance, I forgot where to stand, so the audio levels were low. Afterward, the sound guy was a little upset and scolded me, telling me I should always play close to the mic. It's something I've always remembered, because not much of my playing was captured for the broadcast.

After the show, one of the producers approached me, and instead of handing me a check, he gave me a *Vibe* sweatshirt. And on the way home, not far from the studio, a car pulled up next to me at the stoplight. The driver honked and gave me a thumbs up. My ego loved it; I was a star. And then I realized he was just one of the stagehands from the show.

"Your tail light is out," he said.

I shrank. "Thanks."

And then he added, "Cool song."

It wasn't exactly the paparazzi. The ego is a funny thing; fan it a little, and it comes to life.

Toward the end of my commitment at Camp Kilpatrick, my friend Michelle started coming along with me. She ended up being far more interesting to the fifteen-year-old boys than I was. Not only was Michelle just plain cool, but she was a sword-fighting master and had all sorts of costumes she wore when she did a show.

She was a bit like Uma Thurman's character in the *Kill Bill* films and often performed alongside fire jugglers and other novelty acts. I'm not really sure how it came about, but near the end of my time there, we organized a volunteer talent show.

John played guitar, I played harmonica, and Denise, who was in from Hawaii, played bass. The volunteer jam band played on the basketball court while the Camp Kilpatrick kids watched from the bleachers. Michelle came out in between songs and performed traditional Japanese sword fighting moves.

The best part was that a few of the more confident kids came up to the mic to play a harmonica lick and sing. The boys in the audience were fully engaged and echoed the call and response, which felt powerful and supportive to the boys on the mic. What was especially heartwarming was to watch the staff enjoy it. They knew these kids well, and you could sense the music had shifted something.

About ten years later, I was in a 7-Eleven, and the clerk said to me, "You're Kusala, right?"

"Yes." I was in my civilian clothes.

"You were my music teacher at Camp Kilpatrick," he said.

"I play in a band now because of you."

I was amazed. "What do you play?"

"Drums," he said, "but it all started with the harmonica. I'm in a metal band now."

We caught up a bit and said our goodbyes, and I left with my iced tea, a little disappointed that I'd had anything to do with bringing a heavy metal band into existence. But hey, maybe it kept him out of jail.

Chapter 4
Sickness, Rats, Cats, and Cancer:
The Hospital Chaplain Years 2000-2012

Rain the cat has become the center's mascot in a way. Everyone knows her. She's the only truly domesticated cat of the bunch and comes indoors. She rubs against people while they meditate, and she sleeps with me. Every night she rearranges my room, pushing things off the table and desk. I often wake to a lot of stuff on the floor, and whenever I lose anything, I get down and look under the desk. Every morning around 5:30 a.m., she puts a soft paw on my face, gently telling me she wants to go outside.

One morning when Rain and I came out onto the lawn, I saw Doug, a long-term resident sitting in one of the porch chairs, and I knew something was wrong.

I'd seen Doug sit down only one other time, to tie his shoe. Otherwise, he was up from dawn till dusk maintaining the center's gardens and grounds. And this wasn't because it was his job, he did it out of care for the center. He removed trash that accrued overnight in the yard, thrown over our fence by people in the alley. He picked up cat poop and, depending on who slipped through the fence, sometimes people poop. He cleared general debris from the trees and plants. After tidying the backyard, Doug went out front and walked up and down our block with a bag and a trash picker. He cleaned not only our property but often our neighbors' yards and even the grounds of the apartment building across the street. He was always doing something, usually for the good of the planet or for others. He also didn't really talk all that much.

That morning, he sat in a chair in front of the Quan Yin statue, rake in hand with a freshly shaven head.

Doug had some hearing loss, so it was easy to startle him. Rain broke the ice, trotting ahead of me as we approached.

"Hey, Doug, everything okay?"

He readjusted the rake in his hand. "I got a call around 4 a.m. from Chris," he said. "Reverend Karuna passed away last night at 3:30 a.m."

Reverend Karuna had been the abbess of the center for thirty-four years. She met our founder, Thien An, in the late '70s when she took one of his classes at UCLA for an extended studies credit for her teaching license. She quickly took to Buddhism, finding answers and ideas that gave voice to what she'd always felt.

Karuna means "compassion." She studied under Thien An as a layperson for a few years and helped to start the first meditation group for Westerners at a quaint Hollywood house.

Within a few months, Thien An had the wisdom to realize that Westerners needed Western teachers. He set about creating an educational system that taught traditional Mahayana Buddhism to Westerners who also wanted to teach. He also kept homing in on the value of inclusiveness, building the center on non-denominationalism, which was revolutionary for the times. The center housed many veins of Buddhists, with teachers from traditional Theravadan, Mahayana, Zen, and Tibetan Buddhism. It was quite a colorful block with all the monks walking around in their different robes.

Karuna, by nature, was a wonder. She was strong-willed and asked a lot of questions. Not much slipped her radar, and she was adept at running the center's physical operations, including housing, maintenance, finances, and class logistics. But she also had students of her own who traveled from all parts of the country to study with her. At times she could be heard from a block away reprimanding someone, but the moment her last word was out, she usually dropped the anger. She seemed incapable of holding resentment, and her heart was wide with good intensions, clear with compassion, and grounded by the roots of dharma.

The year prior to her death, she'd moved to Sacramento to receive assisted care in her later years and to be nearer to her family. It was then that Reverend Shanti became the abbot. He's been at the center since the '80s and was the obvious and most supported choice.

Doug tapped the rake on the porch boards. "I guess her last words were, 'That's it.'"

He and I sat quietly in the yard, which Karuna had helped to design. I absorbed the multitude of levels of her last statement. A few years back, a stroke had taken a bit of life from her that she never quite regained, and now she'd passed on at seventy-four. It was painful to think she was gone. Rain pushed against my leg in knowing.

It was about 5:45 a.m., and dawn was upon us. The sky was streaked with long pink veins. Doug rose from the chair. "Behind everything in nature is the ideal thing," he said and then he walked inside.

I didn't know how what he said related to the news, but I knew it did.

Over the next ten days, Reverend Shanti's students came and worked in the yard, cleaned the great hall, and made memorial service arrangements, including speakers, parking, and food. Reverend Shanti contacted all the local monastics, and he was tireless in preparation. When Reverend Karuna's memorial day arrived, about two hundred people showed up.

Around half the attendees were monastics. The colorful litany of religious robes was moving; it embodied the very ideal IBMC was founded on: diversity. It was one of the most meaningful events I'd seen at the center.

A Tibetan Lama came to honor her, as did a high monk for the Vietnamese temple, and monastics from China, India, and Sri Lanka. Four schools were represented, with each tradition coming forward, congregating at her shrine, and chanting in their traditional tongue. There were also Western monks, students of hers, political officials, Catholic representatives, and plain old blue-jean-wearing friends and family, all of whom had much to say about her renegade ways and her effectiveness in running the center.

One particularly interesting story was told by a monk who spoke about how Karuna came under heavy fire for letting drug attics, ex-offenders, and people of "questionable pasts" come to live in the center. She offered the center as a refuge for those who were in need, those coming from abusive relationships, people who had bad credit, the mentally ill, the spiritually sick, and those who suffered deeply on the most basic and profound levels.

A certain high-level monastic called a meeting with her, excoriating her for allowing these misfits in, saying it was creating an unfit environment for monastics to study. She stood right in the man's face and told him that if a monastic were driven away by such an environment, he shouldn't have taken the vows to begin with. She contended that it was actually the best thing for a monastic community, any chance to practice compassion, which is central to the Buddha's teaching.

After the ceremony, there was a lot of food and camaraderie. I noticed that Doug was nowhere to be seen during the ceremony and found him three blocks away, manning the dirt parking lot we'd been allowed to use for the day. He was helping with the overflow parking. I made Doug a plate of food and walked it up to him.

"We missed you down there, Doug," I said.

"Yeah, but if Karuna was here, she'd have put me on parking duty anyhow."

He was right.

I went back to my room and burned incense for Reverend Karuna. She was the person most responsible for me being allowed to live a supported monastic life. She handled my health insurance and stipend, which allowed me to study and practice without the worries that lay people have to face in a materially driven life. I wished her a happy, most favorable rebirth. It was emotional, even with my many hours of Buddhist training on how to die skillfully, and my meditations on death and impermanence. All minds need to grieve; it's part of facing our own inevitable destiny as well as celebrating the shortness and importance of a good life. It's also a necessary part of coming to an acceptance of how things are.

The name Leisure World sounds like a nudist camp, or a place of endless rattan chairs and swimming pools, but it's actually a retirement community and has been one of my favorite places to give talks, especially as I get older. We take Medicare jokes to a new level, and most of the people who live there are happy and busy.

It's an unusually progressive community that hosts a wide array of special interest clubs, including the Buddhist Circle, which was often well attended. I appreciated the group's pizzazz. I was often introduced with a sort of show business professionalism that included a band or keyboardist who played me on stage. L.A. breeds a lot of that.

Another organization at Leisure World was the Audio Visual Club, which filmed an interview that the event organizer, Lynn, conducted with me, and which was broadcast on the Leisure World cable TV channel, replete with snazzy graphics.

One Saturday after a talk, I noticed that one of the regular attendees was absent. I asked Lynn about Helen and learned that her brain cancer had returned, and she wasn't feeling up to coming. The following month, Lynn relayed a message from Helen asking me to pay her a visit, so I did.

Helen had had a British husband for most of her life. He'd passed away long ago, but her speech was still peppered with British phrases even though she was from Iowa. Her apartment was on the periphery of Leisure World, and when I knocked on the door, a nurse answered.

This was Helen's third go round with the same cancer, and she wasn't looking good. The first time, she was clear for a few years; the second time, she was in remission for a few months; and now, well, she looked tired, and the doctors were suggesting a treatment that was still in testing, one that had some known side effects and a lot of unknown ones too. The other option was to do nothing and pass away in palliative care.

"Hey there, Helen," I said, as the nurse showed me into the living room.

The chemo had taken her hair, and she was wearing a wig. She sat at the window with a crossword on her lap.

"Come in, dear, come sit," she said, sparking to life. She waved me toward her. "How was the talk?"

I brought a chair over. "It was fine, but we missed you."

I noticed a blurry old tattoo on her foot. I had no idea who Helen really was; all I knew was that she liked Buddhist talks and sat in the third row. We'd spoken once or twice about her son, who was an artist, but today she wasn't looking like herself. The nurse left, and Helen sat staring out the window as the late morning sun filtered in.

"The one cloud over there, it doesn't move with the others," she said, pointing toward the hills where a small cloud sat low, crowning the hillside.

"It's just been staring at me through the window all morning."

"I bet the house under the cloud is wondering what the heck is up," I said.

A tea kettle chirped from the stove.

"They say I'm not to have tea, but I may be about to exit anyway, and a little tea never hurried it along."

"Probably not," I agreed.

"Would you like some tea, dear?" she asked.

"Tea sounds nice," I said.

Helen stood with the help of her walker. She pushed her way over to the stove in a series of three-step movements and carefully poured the hot water.

"Be right back," she said as she made her way to the bathroom. She disappeared for a long while, and after a bit of a ruckus, I said, "You okay?"

She spoke through the door. "Never ask a woman in the bathroom if she's okay. It's plain rude, dear."

After a long minute of further struggling, she emerged. I stood and brought the tea over.

"So you're the Buddhist monk, right?" she said.

I was surprised she was unsure, but sickness and age can affect a person.

"Yep." I sipped the tea.

"Well, I'm in a bit of a twist, so I'm interviewing all the holy people I can find."

"Oh?"

"I'm not sure how to die. I've got two options." she said, exhaling. "I've already gone through two surgeries and chemo with the last go round, and this new stuff, it's harsh, and they don't really know if it'll work. It sounds like they have me walking circles around an open grave until we see which topples me first, the meds or the cancer. Or I can do nothing. Then I've got about a month."

Helen's face collapsed for a millisecond, her fear and suffering streaking through her eyes.

I glanced away, feeling a pang of sadness for her. The small cloud still hovered as the others glided on above it. We sat for a moment, surrounded by the quandary.

"That's a pretty hard decision," I said, swallowing.

"Isn't it?" she said.

One of her two beautiful cats appeared and pushed against the leg of her chair.

"This is Betsy," she said.

I bent to pet her, and another cat poked around the edge of the blanket.

"That's Debbie."

Both were calicos and beautiful.

They darted away.

"Well, what do you think I should do?" she said quietly.

I put down my tea.

"It doesn't matter what I would do, Helen; it's what you want."

"Every one of you religious people says that. I'm here trapped on a rock in the middle of the ocean, and can't one of you just answer the darn question?"

"Who else have you asked?"

She sighed. "I've had the Catholic, a rabbi, and a pastor over for tea, and no one can give me a straight answer."

Her wry sense of awareness took me by surprise. Although she carried herself with worldly confidence, there was a look of frailty in all her corners now.

"Well." I felt useless. "I don't know," I said.

"That's not an answer," she mumbled.

"Actually, in Zen Buddhism, 'I don't know' is an answer. We really don't know anything. We just have opinions."

We shared a smile.

"I think it's best if you listen to the doctor," I said. "This is more of a medical question than a religious one."

Something in the air cleared, and she nodded in agreement. Then she looked out the window again and bit her lower lip.

"You know, Helen, the religious question here is how you're going to die. It's the most important thing we ever do."

"The pastor says I'll still get into heaven even if it is very last minute."

"That's pretty foolproof then," I said.

"What if he's wrong?"

She pointed to my full tea cup. "You're letting it get cold. Don't you like it?"

I looked at the tea. "Not all that much," I said with a smile.

She smiled too. "You've always said it like it is, Kusala, from the stage or wherever."

"I say it like it is for me," I said. "I'm not a big fan of L.A. tap water."

"Yeah, it gives brain cancer." She turned her face to the sun coming through the window and closed her eyes. "I'll miss this." Then she sat quietly. "I've got a few days to decide. When are you coming back?"

"I'm here every month." The words bounced around the room and rolled under the couch. I'd forgotten that she was in a different time frame.

"Oh," she said. "Can I call you?"

"Helen, you can call me every day. I can come back too if you'd like, but you have to invite me..."

She smiled.

"...and don't make me tap water tea," I joked.

"Well, I've got the rabbi coming tomorrow. I may go with him for this whole thing, so I'll let you know," she said wryly. "But if you come up with any, well, actual opinions on the situation, do let me know."

"The thing about opinions is they always change as we grow."

"You're no help at all," she said, poking my arm.

I started to gather my things. We said our goodbyes, and I gave her my cell number in case she wanted to call.

I'd wanted a better answer for her, but there was no googling this sort of thing. We had to sit with the fact that there were no answers. I didn't try to give any or find any. My job was to just to show up and listen. Over the course of all the community volunteering I've done, it was always helpful for me to remember that. What I say and do is just a small part of the larger situation. There were causes far and wide that played into everything.

Helen called the next day to invite me to come over. When I arrived, she was sitting at the same window, and Debbie was in her lap.

"The rabbi came," she said.

"Any new thoughts from you?"

"I hate to say it, Helen, but my answer really has no bearing on your predicament, because it would be all about me. Each person has their own karma, so we all have to work out our destiny. I can tell you what I would do, but it might not be useful in your life."

"You're the first to say that," she said. "The Catholic, the Christian, and the rest of them say they're going home to God, and won't heaven be wonderful? Minus the rabbi, who was vague about the afterlife in the Jewish tradition."

"Oh? I thought you said nobody had any answers for you."

"I was just pressuring you to come up with something. It seems all these holy people were talking about their kinship with God," she said.

I paused, trying to be politically correct. "There's value in all ways of thinking, because every religion works at some level. Two sides of the same coin, just different coins."

"You're still not very much help," she said.

"What did the doctors say?" I asked.

"They're pretty neutral, but I think they'd like me to do the treatment so they can log further studies on the drug."

"Oh," I said.

"My mom only talked about God when something went wrong, and my father always said the government put God on the dollar so that we'd all feel better about paying taxes. But that's about it. I feel late to the game," she said with a tinge of sadness.

"Helen, there is no late; it's all just unfolding as it is. That's all. I think the most valuable thing is simple awareness."

"Bullocks," she said.

"It's good you have the ability and time to think; some people never do. And their denial of death can cause terror. If there's one thing I can stress, it's to try and have a peaceful passing."

We sat for a few moments.

"But those Buddhist robes you wear, I don't do brown," she joked.

"I'm not here to convert you. We don't do that," I said.

"Soft sell, huh?"

"I've got to get back to the center for meditation," I said. "But whatever you do, it's your choice."

She glanced out the window.

"That cloud is gone," she said quietly.

I sat down again, not knowing what else to say. "Do you want me to come again tomorrow?"

"That's very generous, but I need some space, dear."

She smiled. "I've got some thinking to do."

I reached into my bag and pulled out a paper sack.

"I got it at the farmer's market. It's real chai tea."

She smelled it. "Brilliant," she said, clutching the bag. "Is that why you monks are so poor all the time? You buy sick people things?"

I laughed.

When I left, traffic had gotten heavy early, but the HOV lane was wide open. I was grateful for the sunshine. And as I zipped by the bumper-to-bumper line of cars, I was even more grateful to be on the motorcycle.

One of our tenants at the center—Deadra, we'll call her—was always a wild card. You never knew what was going to come out of her mouth. Sometimes it was something off-handedly wise, and other times it was a slew of cuss words that didn't even make sense. The one thing you could count on was that she was going to be loud. She spoke loudly, walked loudly, and sang loudly "to herself." I'm not sure where she came from or how she found the center, but she moved into the smallest room on the property in Quan Yin almost a year ago. She'd been raised by her grandmother and was working toward getting her GED.

Often I'd see her perched on the porch steps reading her Bible, or in the backyard chanting Hindu mantras while throwing rose petals at certain cats she thought needed blessings.

One day, Deadra came outside singing the newest Beyonce song and crossed the yard toward the koi pond where I was sitting. "What's up, Reverend Kusala?"

"Not a lot, just watching fish. How about you?"

"I applied for a job at the suit place, Men's Wearhouse. It was a seriously long application."

"Guess that weeds out lazy people from the get-go."

"I hope they call."

I would bet she had to hope for lots of things in her life.

"That job, talking with men all day, helping them pick out suits—what could be better? "

Deadra's laugh was a catch-22, at once infectious and vexingly loud. It was the kind of laugh that came from the gut, very real, very honest. It could get you laughing right alongside her, but the problem was, that encouraged her to go on and on (and on and on).

"We've got a huge rat in the house," she said, squishing her face. "It shits Tic-Tac-sized poops. We need to set some traps out, but Doug refuses to get 'em. It could give us diseases."

"Hate to break it to you," I said, "but nobody's going to kill it."

"I'll kill it then. I'll blow that mother up."

I shook my head. "The center wouldn't take kindly to that. We don't kill things here."

"I had to bag up everyone's food in the cupboards," she said. "People are freaked out."

Turns out that nobody in the house was freaked out except her.

"I'll talk to Doug," I said and walked over to the Quan Yin House.

Doug was already on it and had ordered live traps from Amazon, but this rat ended up being either smart or plain strong. There were no signs of him except for his poop, but the cheese and peanut butter disappeared every night without a trace.

A few days later, I was two houses down when I heard Deadra scream. She'd seen the rat on the floor and claimed it was the size of toy poodle. After that, Deadra started wearing boots in the house, and it was horribly loud for everyone. She was terrified that the rat would get into her room, so she sprayed Raid on the threshold of her doorway. She also sprayed the food cabinets in the kitchen. She was told that she'd be asked to leave if she did that again, as the other roommates weren't comfortable with toxins in food areas.

One night a pipe broke in the basement, and the rat was seen swimming about. When the plumber arrived, he found the rat sitting in the basement sink. It was so big and slow, he just picked it up by the tail, took it outside to the trunk of his car, and let it go in an alley across town.

When Deadra found out, she was skeptical. "Rats have radar," she said. "It'll find its way back." She seemed to need to see its dead body in order to feel safe.

"He's in Brentwood now," I said. "I'm sure he's happier there—better food and more of it. Organic."

"I think this is one of his hairs," she said, holding a strand that looked more like a thread than a hair.

"Could be one of yours," I said. She did have short black hair.

"I'd know my own hair," she said. "The damn rat is back."

It wasn't enough to tell her it was gone. We had to show her. Night after night, we put out traps with peanut butter and cheese, and night after night, it went untouched except for the mass of ants the bait attracted. Finally Deadra gave up, and we never heard another word about it. I find it funny that people have a thing against rats. The human psyche is a rather complicated mess for us all to unwind.

Back at Leisure World, Helen had bigger things to think about.

"I'm not doing the new chemo cocktail," she told me on the phone.

"You feel okay about it?"

She paused. "I do."

And I believed her.

"I'd like you to counsel me through this," she said. "I need you to help me let go."

"There's no formula, but we can do it together."

She fell silent, and I think she was crying.

"It's strange to think that every day I'm only getting worse. I can never get better than yesterday."

"Helen, sick or not, tomorrow I'll be one day older too. After a certain age, today is the best we'll ever have."

She blew her nose.

"I'd like to die 'skillfully,' as you put it."

"I'll do my best to help, but the hospice people are trained, and I'm not."

With that, Helen set out to accept the inevitable. A woman from UCLA came to help her with her will. We spoke often on the phone, and I visited. Every time I saw her, she was a bit weaker but also less stressed. We discussed her daughter, and Helen came to understand that she didn't need to worry about her; she'd raised a very capable woman who could carry on without her, just as Helen had done when her own mother had passed.

The interconnected web of life helps people know that nobody ever stands alone; we're always in relationship to each other, forever.

As I was getting ready to go visit Helen one morning, I received a text from Lynn that Helen was gone. I burned some incense and recited the Maranassati sutta, which talks about death in rather a poetic way. I was glad Helen was out of this life and had a feeling she'd find a wonderful cup of tea in the next.

Joe, on the other hand, he was a harder case.

I received a call from the Veteran's Administration Hospital one afternoon. They said that a patient was requesting me, but his name didn't ring a bell.

The V.A. medical facility was a newer building on the west side, off Wilshire. I'd never been there and was surprised by its size. A super-sized American flag hung at the entrance, and when the elevator doors opened onto Joe's wing, it was a bit eerie. The patriotic décor of red, white, and blue suggested a 4th of July cookout, but a deep sadness permeated the place. There were only men in Joe's wing, and all of them were struggling. Some hobbled on prosthetics; others pushed walkers. It was too quiet for a place with so many people. I asked where the palliative care was, and as the nurse walked me to Joe's room, I felt uneasy. I figured Joe and I must have met at some point, but I had no recollection of the man I was about to see. I hoped I would remember him, but if I didn't, I would just tell him right off the bat, like I always did. It gave people a second chance at a first impression.

The nurse tapped on the door to see if Joe was awake.

Inside, Joe lay with his eyes closed, listening to the TV. Although he had bandages on his face, I recognized him immediately from our Wednesday night meditations at the center.

He'd started coming a few years back and was always quiet, never said much. I was happy that the sangha had accepted him so warmly. I'm not sure which war he served in, but his wrinkles were deep, his skin tanned. He had the wiry frame of someone who slept outside and didn't have enough food. Even so, he always put some dana in the box, even if it was only coins. I hadn't noticed when Joe stopped coming to meditation, as people regularly came and went. But now, seeing him lying there brought back my fondness for him. I was honored he'd asked for me to come. He was dying of skin cancer.

The nurse left and I took a seat in the corner. He had a private room, no personal effects, no cards or balloons, just multiple bracelets and tags that hung from his IV like a coupon book. He seemed to be breathing smoothly, though.

Joe opened his eyes and stared at me. "I'm dying."

His voice said it all. It was strained, dry, raspy.

I nodded and pulled a chair over to his bed. He had little energy for niceties. Joe wasn't interested in being friends; he was only interested in how to die skillfully.

"You know," I said, "there are hospice workers who are better trained than I, but we can talk about it, if that's okay?"

He nodded.

"I remember you coming to the center all those times

for meditation, which is a better start than most people ever get. In a way, you already have some practice dying."

Joe smiled as best he could.

"When we meditate, we're really letting go of everything for fifteen minutes—our laundry, pets, relationships. Death is letting go of everything forever."

He closed his eyes.

"I always liked your cat," he said.

"Rain's still around."

"It's hard to meditate with all the drugs."

"You always have the right to ask for less medication, but I would talk to the doctors about that. I'm not in a position to give medical advice. What you've done in your past with meditation is still with you, Joe, drugs or not. It's never gonna go away."

"What do I do as I die?" he asked.

I paused, unsure of what to say. "I think the simplest thing would be to watch your breath."

Joe was quiet.

"What we want to do is focus on the present moment, and every sensation we have, like the breath sensation that's happening right now. It's not about fixating on the future, because there isn't one, and it's not about regretting the past, because it no longer matters. It's about coming to the present moment, experiencing your life right now. The sensation of breath is the doorway."

Joe was still quiet.

"Do you want some water?" I asked.

He shook his head no.

"What happens when I'm gone?"

"Well, in Buddhism, they say the last thought in this lifetime is the first one in the next life, so as we take our last breath, it's good to recall all the generosity and kindness and compassion in your life. It helps with a skillful transition into a heaven realm. But in Buddhism, heaven isn't forever, because whatever karma got you to heaven will eventually wear out. And heaven can be up to one hundred thousand human lifetimes long, but there's no way of creating new karma there, so you come back into a human form for another lifetime to start working on your karma account again."

Joe shifted without saying anything.

"The center holds a Ullambana ceremony every year, and we'll read your name along with the names of all the other people who have passed on this year. We also offer food, money, and clothing to departed spirits. It's a way of keeping them alive in our hearts. Nobody is truly dead until the last person who knew your name has passed on. We also read parts of the Ullambana Sutra."

I didn't mention that the ceremony was for trapped spirits in the hell realm.

"I'd like permission to include your picture on the center's memorial alter in the zendo, if that's okay?"

"Why?" he said. "I didn't come much."

"That doesn't matter. Your picture on the wall will help people remember the eminence of death."

Joe nodded. "Okay, yeah then."

I got the feeling that everything Joe owned was in the closet of his hospital room and that I was going to be the only visitor.

Joe closed his eyes. I felt sad but reminded myself that we're all interconnected, even in aloneness, which was different than loneliness. Still, I was relieved when he fell asleep.

I left the building feeling more emotional than I'd expected and sat on a bench in the courtyard, the big American flag waving overhead in the afternoon wind. I took in the air and hoped for Joe to pass quietly and easily, without suffering.

I felt strange on that bench; my brown robes clashed with all the red, white, and blue. Visitors streamed past like carnival goers, some with gifts and flowers. I got a lot of looks, and many felt oddly respectful. I'm not sure why. Maybe they thought I was Catholic.

The following morning was beautiful, and the traffic to South Central L.A. was light for a Friday. I'd been asked to speak to high school students at a private Catholic school, so instead of going in early, I sat in the car listening to NPR: More bombings in the Middle East, and the economy had taken a sharp dip at day's end. There was also a study out about how to drink without getting a hangover. People amaze me.

I went to the front office, checked in, got my name tag. When the bell rang, kids poured out into the hallways like ants from an anthill. I made my way toward room 126. Bernadette was an old friend and had taught world religions at the school for close to twenty years. My talk had become an annual part of her syllabus, and this was the eighth or ninth time. I rather enjoyed the energy of scholastic youths and always looked forward to it.

Grokking was a term I first encountered in the '70s book *Stranger in a Strange Land*, by Robert Heinlein. It references a type of awareness of one's environment. Essentially it's the opposite of what most public speakers are trained to do. Rather than trying to understand who the audience is based on clothing, background, and other factors, grokking requires one to open up to the timbre and presence in the room. Rather than understanding the audience, I "feel" the audience, so to speak. If you speak to an audience's hearts, you speak to everyone, but when you speak to the intellect, you're likely leaving someone out. When your grock meter has an off day, though, it can be a struggle.

I opened with a song, and then I began the talk with my usual: "In Buddhism, God is optional..." I was trying to be inclusive of atheists, theists, and non-theists, but what came out instead was, "In Buddhism, the concept of God less important than the concept of suffering." While this is actually true for a lot of Buddhist practitioners, it's not an appropriate thing to say to young adults who've been taught their relationship with God is important. So I tried another tack.

"The reason we don't do the God theory is that Buddhism is about how and why we suffer and how to end it."

A student's hand went up. "What's faith?" she asked.

"Well, we do have faith, but it means that we believe there was a human who became perfect, and we call him the Buddha. So faith for a Buddhist would be necessary for the first step. The second step is when faith turns into confidence, because the teachings self-validate."

Bernadette smiled.

"So you're saying there's no God?" someone asked.

"I'm saying there are gods, and the Buddha believed in the gods of his time, many gods. But he came to realize they couldn't or wouldn't end worldly discomfort. So that's when he rediscovered the path to end human suffering."

Another hand went up. "Do Buddhists believe in the Big Bang?"

"We're not really concerned with how everything started. In fact, in Buddhism, there is no first cause. It's always been here, always will be, and is constantly changing."

"Can you say that again?"

These kids were smart and relentless.

"It's not important how it all started; it's about what we're doing now that counts."

I could see their mental hard drives were spinning and stuck, like a whirling rainbow beachball of doom. Nothing was processing.

"Where's Nirvana?" someone asked.

"It's something you realize, not someplace you go. The Buddhist practice doesn't take us any place. It helps us realize we're already there."

"Where?" a kid asked.

"It's not a where. It's actually a place that's inside any one of us. It's not an outside place."

"But there are so many bad things in the world. How could you not suffer if you're here?"

"Good question. That's the point. A Buddhist feels they can't change the world, they can change only themselves, and if enough people change themselves, the world changes too. We're all connected. The world isn't all out there; we experience it as a community, a group, a population."

They looked down, pencils in hand, unsure what notes to take.

"Buddhism isn't about what's on page thirty-four in some book. Buddhism is based on how you experience the world, which is always different than your neighbor. So it's really an empirical practice."

"How do you know if someone is enlightened?" a girl asked.

"There are four things that enlightened people do: They always have the intention of kindness, which manifests in the activity of compassion. They no longer find success or happiness only in their own life, but they find it in the lives of others. They feel the happiness and success of others as if it's their own. The fourth thing is equanimity, which comes from realizing how all things are interconnected and interdependent. So nothing stands apart or alone."

"What's the difference between kindness and compassion?"

"Kindness is the intention or motivation behind compassion, and compassion is the activity that reduces suffering in the world. Compassion changes the world; kindness changes you."

I watched their brains power down and give up. "It's not easy to explain."

"Isn't that what you're supposed to do?" a student said.

Everyone laughed, including me.

"Put it this way," I said. "An enlightened person probably won't say that they are enlightened and won't be wearing cool shoes either."

A few kids laughed, but I don't think they knew why.

I wrapped up the day with a song on my harmonica, and everyone left more or less happy.

When I got back to the center, I remembered we had a picture of Joe. It was taken during a sangha celebration. After a short search, I found it, plus a candid one of Joe and Rain the cat on a chair. I made copies and brought them to the hospital on my next visit. I also brought a small plastic box that looked like a radio and plays Buddhist prayers, some incense, and a small Buddha statue. Joe looked at the pictures for a while.

"Can you get me some tape?" he asked.

I borrowed some from the nurse's station and watched Joe struggle as he tried to affix the pictures to his IV stand.

When I tried to help, he said, "I got it!"

I sat back down. When he finally got them up, he looked exhausted.

"Can we turn off the TV?" I asked.

He nodded. The silence was deafening.

"I like that Buddha, thanks," he said.

"I thought the chanting box might also be nice instead of the TV sometimes."

He nodded and lowered the bed into a flat position and fell right to sleep. Taping up those pictures had tired him out. I left the chants playing.

I got a call three days later from a nurse saying that Joe was not doing well, and when I arrived, the picture of Joe and Rain had been taped to the outside of his door. I later learned that nurses will sometimes do that as a way to connect with whoever they are caring for; it gives the patient an identity beyond being sick. I found it compassionate.

"You must be Kusala," a voice said from the hallway.

I turned around.

"I'm Todd, Joe's brother."

He looked just like Joe.

"He passed about ten minutes ago," Todd said.

He had arrived late the night before, and thankfully was with Joe when he went. But there was no mention of other family members or a memorial service. When I said my condolences, I teared up a little. Embarrassed, I apologized.

"I'm glad Joe knew you," Todd said. "He didn't have many friends. "

I nodded.

"I'm relieved that you were with him."

"He went rather quietly. We had the chanting box on. It seemed to help him relax."

I looked at the picture taped to the door. There was really nothing else to say. Todd and I parted ways, and I left without going into Joe's room. It always strikes me how we're here one moment, and then our voice disappears forever. Impermanence, an engine that sits idling in every corner of the universe.

When I got back to the center, I found Carl lying on his stomach on the backyard footpath. He had something trapped under a water glass.

"Special K, come here. Look at this. I found this under a rock over there."

I hunched over and looked through the glass. A black quarter-size beetle stood in all its stink bug glory. It was pushing against the side of the glass, trying to escape.

"Maybe put him back? He's probably hungry," I said.

"No, I've got potato chips for him." Carl shook the snack-size bag and shoved one under the glass.

The bug froze.

"I don't think they eat those," I said. "He wants out. See what he's doing?"

"He doesn't even know he's in there."

"I think he does, and he wants out," I said.

Carl lifted the glass off like a magician, but the beetle didn't move. It just sat there. So Carl promptly replaced the glass.

"See," he said. "It doesn't even know it's in there."

The beetle moved toward the perimeter of the glass again and reassumed its prodding.

"It'll die under there," I said.

"It'll die anyway."

I thought of Joe.

The bug moved along the glass's perimeter.

"It's free!" Carl said, lifting the glass again with dramatic flair.

"Leave it alone," I said, walking away. "Put it back where you found it."

Later, when I was out feeding the cats, I noticed the beetle was still there. Maybe it was dead. Maybe it wasn't. The next morning it was gone.

A few days later, I got a call from the UCLA Care Committee telling me there was a woman who was awaiting a liver transplant. She'd requested me by name, although we'd never met. I guess she'd found me through an article. The funny thing was, she wasn't a Buddhist.

Karen was forty-seven and gaunt. She wasn't a drinker, which accounted for her high ranking on the transplant list. She was in need because of a genetic condition.

Karen wanted to talk, but she was in pain and remained pretty quiet. I did most of the talking, asking her questions she could answer with a nod or the shake of her head. Her husband arrived along with a doctor shortly after me.

He introduced himself to me. "Jack," he said, pumping my hand. He seemed to be expecting me.

I stepped to the back as the doctor assessed the paperwork. "The good news is, your kidneys are responding," the doctor said.

Jack shifted uneasily.

"So does that put her on lower on the transplant list then?"

The doctor's eyes dropped back down to his paperwork as he composed words. "Lower isn't really the right word," he said tactfully. "It just puts her in a different need category. But your advocate knows the ins and outs of all that. I don't want to misinform you. Is your advocate in today?"

Jack looked at Karen, who couldn't say more than a few words.

"If it's Tuesday," Jack said, rubbing his tired eyes.

The doctor replaced the chart. "I'll be sure she comes in."

It was a hell of a situation to be in. If Karen improved, she dropped on the transplant list. If she worsened, she gained ground. But there was no certainty that a liver would be available when Karen needed it. It's a horrible catch-22, and Karen's husband looked like he'd soon be in a bed next to her recovering from a heart attack. Stress can be severe on caregivers. I'm more helpful to them than to the sick sometimes. It's a huge help if I'm there visiting when they need to go home. Leaving a patient all alone can be harder on the caregiver than on the patient.

Karen seemed to take the news in stride, but Jack looked worried. The advocate was a warm and compassionate person but looked oddly young for her age, like a candy striper volunteer or something. She was armed with a pencil and a clipboard. I peered over her shoulder and half expected to see a tennis ladder schematic on her paperwork, lines connecting upward, sending a liver here or there if this person got better.

The advocate said Karen would retain a "top tier position " but that she'd still remain in the same category. The answer felt like an auto-responder email, a letdown of sorts, even though it shouldn't have.

Jack and Karen had children, so when Jack left to pick them up from school, he asked me to stay longer.

Over the years, I've come to sense when death is circling

someone's bedside, and there looked to be footprints around Karen's bed. With her husband gone, she was able to talk a little more openly about why she'd called. A few years back, I'd done a memorial service for her friend, and she wanted to ask if I would do hers. She hadn't talked to her husband about it yet.

"It'd be an honor to do it, as long as Jack's okay with it," I told her.

She nodded gratefully and tears filled her eyes. Karen was tired. Her genetic condition had her sick for years. She was being realistic. The chances were low a liver would come in time.

"Is there anything I can do?" I asked.

A tear popped out of her eye and slid down her cheek. She looked away.

"Maybe a liver will come in," I said.

She only nodded.

We were quiet.

"I'm not Buddhist," she finally said.

"That makes no difference."

"What do you think happens when you die?" she asked.

"Of course, nobody knows, but in Buddhism, we have a variety of answers. I have confidence in rebirth."

"I liked what you said at the service, that we are all traveling through it together."

I couldn't remember who her friend was, but it didn't matter.

Jack arrived back within the hour and I left them both smiling, somehow.

It's hard to know what to say to someone who is dying, especially to those who've never given any real thought to the process or what may lie beyond. And there are a lot of people out there who weren't raised with any ideas about religion. It's just so important to be free of regret as they continue.

A few days later, I arrived back at Karen's room with a pen and paper to discuss memorial plans, only to find she'd been moved to hospice. Jack made it clear that it was only for insurance reasons. "Once she gets the liver, she'll get moved back into the main wing," he said. Jack went home for a nap, and I took a seat, enjoying the quiet while Karen slept.

"Kusala," she said, waking up. Karen didn't look good; her eyes weren't moving normally.

I thought of a book I'd read once that said sometimes when people die slowly, it's like a Nordic tide, inching out a little at a time until the floating boat sits beached and useless. She was still afloat but in the shallowest of waters.

I sat with her. We said very little. It was springtime, and it didn't seem right to have so much budding life just outside her window.

When Karen's sister, Kim, arrived, she walked to the hospital room, dropped the two large paper bags on the counter like it was her kitchen, and then bee-lined straight to the bathroom. She didn't look anything like Karen, but then again, I really didn't know what Karen looked like with a healthy liver.

Kim yelled to us from the bathroom, "I thought I'd explode. I've been holding it since Hollywood!"

She emerged far more relaxed and began to wipe Karen's lips with a damp paper towel.

"You hungry?" she asked.

Karen shook her head.

"They didn't have any potato salad," Kim said matter of factly, pulling up a chair and biting into a pumpernickel sandwich.

"Who are you?" she asked me.

"Karen and I are friends," I said. "We met a while back."

Kim shrugged off the fact that I was a monastic in a brown robe and asked me about local restaurants in the area. I had a meeting back at the center, so I said my goodbyes and left.

The next day, Kim put a PayPal link up on Facebook where people could donate money to help with medical costs. It's strange to think that somewhere in the transplant patient paperwork, there's a line item that says "liver" with a price next to it. This way of getting financial help is great for people; it's bad enough that they're emotionally put through the wringer, but bankruptcy is a common part of the sickness story.

At the end of the month, if Karen didn't get a liver, they were going to move her back to Milwaukee, where there was a shorter donor list.

I came to find out that Karen was a singer, and although she'd never gotten a Grammy, she'd been nominated for several. She was really good, a blend of blues and gospel.

Toward the end of the month, Karen still had no liver. She was starting to fade, and I saw her giving up. She didn't want to be moved back to Milwaukee and felt the trip would kill her.

"Come on, if you go back to Milwaukee, you could be near the studio," her sister kept saying. "You've got the next record half done. You can write the rest while you're recuperating."

Jack, Karen, and I were silent.

The following day, her sister called me on the phone.

"Hi," she said oddly.

"Hi. Everything okay?"

"You know we really love Karen," she said.

"I can tell; you two seem close."

"Well, that's what we…I mean I…speaking on behalf of our family…wanted to talk to you about."

I kicked off my shoes and sat back in my desk chair with a feeling of nervousness.

"Somewhere, Karen got the idea that going to Milwaukee wasn't a good idea."

I paused, recalling there was no manual for this circumstance.

"Yes, I heard she's opted to stay in L.A.," I said.

"Well, Kusala, she's gonna die if she stays. We're all wondering how she got the idea."

I didn't know what to say, but through the phone I felt a finger pointing into my chest.

"It must be a hard thing to decide," I said. "She expressed concern about the trip to me, and asked me what I thought, but all I could tell her was that this was a medical decision, not a religious one, so there was nothing I could offer in the form of opinion."

"She also somehow seems to think that doing her will and pre-buying her funeral services is a good idea," said Kim.

I ran my hand down Rain the cat's back.

"Karen isn't ready to die," Kim said.

"I'm not sure anyone is," I said.

In the background, I heard a door open and close, and Kim became more abrupt. "Listen, we love her, and we think the drugs have made her depressed. We need everyone to help her rally."

"It's a hard situation any way you slice it," I said.

"Are you the one who brought her the Buddha statue?" Kim asked.

"She requested it," I said.

"She's obsessed with that thing! She's had me move it from here to there in the hospital room."

I sat silent. There was nothing I could say that would be right.

"Can you tell her to just go to Milwaukee?" she said point-blank.

"This is up to her. I don't have any advice for this sort of thing. I don't tell people what to do, I just encourage people to think about things in a variety of ways, and none of them are ultimately right. There's no right answer."

If there was ever a pregnant pause, this one was with twins.

"What good are you? Why can't you just tell her what to do?" she screamed.

I was quiet, and Kim broke into a crying jag. Her pain sliced through the telephone and into my chest. I was filled with sadness for her, and for Karen.

"There's no right answer; grief is unbearable," I said, trying to soothe her.

"If you can't help us, could you at least just not come for a while? We'd love to surround her with people who are supportive," she said.

It felt like a bind. Karen had asked me to come, Kim was asking me not to.

"I'm a Chaplain. It's my job to honor her wishes."

"She's sick. She has no idea what she wants," Kim sobbed.

"I can't go in with an agenda. All I can do is help her in whatever way she asks."

"It's easy for you to say; you've only known her ten minutes."

"You're right." I paused. "I think that's part of why she asked me to come."

There was only silence. And more of it.

"I try to avoid opinions and just give her my fullest attention," I reiterated.

"Give me a break on that mindfulness stuff," she said between sobs. "What good is it for her to be here now, with this? We want it to be different."

Kim hung up, and that was that.

I thought about her question: what good is mindfulness in the midst of suffering? And I was reminded of what Ram Das taught. Being here now is the only place we can be; the future hasn't happened, and the past is over. That's where all the work is, in the now. You have to know fear to also know fearlessness.

Last week, Karen had requested that I bring some quotes for her memorial service. As I walked down the hospital hall toward her room, I stopped at the nurse's station.

The nurse took a breath and looked at me.

"Kusala, they've put you on the list of no visitors. I'm sorry."

She stared at me.

I felt really strange, like someone had taken something dear from me.

"Oh," I said, looking down at the paperwork in my hand. "Karen wanted these."

This nurse knew me well. Her eyes said no to the paperwork. I exhaled.

"I'm sorry, Kusala. Karen...she requested you on the list too."

This was confusing. I'd been asked to come, and now unasked. Monk or not, rejection isn't easy.

I gave the nurse a nod and went into the volunteers' lounge. One of the Catholic chaplains stood picking over the snacks. He always seemed to be in there; lots of Catholics die, it seems.

"How's it going, Kusala?" he said, cookie in hand.

"Lots of suffering," I said, shaking my head.

"Me too." Crumbs dropped on his robe as he chewed.

"I just got booted out of a room," I said.

"Wow, what happened?" he said, pulling up a chair.

We sat and talked about it. He reminded me that sick people are sick, and families can't be counted on for rational behavior.

The lounge door pushed open again, and the nurse from the hallway poked her head in.

"You okay?" she asked.

"So he's really blacklisted?" the Catholic blurted.

"If it means anything, Karen's husband wasn't supportive of this move, Kusala."

"It's okay," I said, collecting my things.

I was surprised to get a call from Jack a few months later. Karen had gotten a liver. However, there were complications, and she'd passed away. He wanted me to know that she'd died with the Buddha statue on her bedside table and the chant box I'd given her taped to her bible.

"She covered all the bases," Jack said. "We replaced that battery in the chant box once a week. She slept with it on. It was playing when she passed."

I never asked about the end-of-life paperwork, and they never asked me to perform the service that Karen had requested. I just gave her prayers for forty-nine days, put her picture on the memorial altar, and included her on the roster at IBMC's annual Ullambana ceremony.

It was an average afternoon for me, but little Leo the cat was having a hard time. He was the underdog among the cats, the scrawniest and skinniest of them all. That day he showed up oddly dirty, mud caked all over him, and he couldn't open one eye. He looked like he'd been in the wrong place at the wrong time, and a bus had come by and splashed a mud puddle all over him.

He moved in pain, so I picked him up and brought him inside. The old adage that cats and water don't mix couldn't be more correct, and as I started wiping off the mud with a damp towel, he latched his mouth onto my index finger and bit down hard. Little Leo left three puncture holes with sentiment.

I couldn't blame him; it probably hurt as I pulled the mud clods from his fur. I finished washing him and took care of my finger by rinsing the bite. That night, he was back outside eating dinner, hungry and happy.

Three days later, I awoke to not just a swollen finger but a swollen hand. It looked like the Michelin Man's hand, swollen up the wrist. The holes were oozing puss. I called the doctor, and he said I had to go to the ER immediately.

"Cat bites lead nowhere good," he said. "Let's get it checked out."

I went in that afternoon.

The first doctor took one look and sent me across the street to an orthopedist. That doctor took another look and said I needed surgery the next morning.

"Surgery?" I stalled. "Really?"

"If we don't open the finger and drain it, there's a potential of sepsis. I've seen people lose a whole hand. It's rare, but feline infections can turn for the worse in a matter of hours. Their mouths are really dirty," he said, shaking his head and scribbling something down on my paperwork.

I pictured little Leo with a dead L.A. rat hanging from his mouth. Dirty.

"The surgery won't take long, but we'll keep you overnight for observation and give you IV antibiotics. You'll have to stay."

I rolled down my sleeve in shock, nodded, and went back to the center.

That night at meditation, everyone was asking about the large bandage on my hand, and when I told them the story, it seemed everyone but me knew cat bites could go south. Rebecca asked if I needed a ride to surgery, and I guess I did.

We arrived at the hospital the next morning, but Rebecca had a fear of parking garages and germs, so she pulled over a few blocks away from the hospital and said that was as far as she'd go.

"Sorry," she said without sounding very sorry. "Plus I've got stuff I gotta do."

"Oh, okay," I said as I got out of the car. "Thanks."

"Good luck," she said and dropped the car into drive.

I stood on the corner of Sunset and Vermont and stared at the large hospital down the way. On the other side of the street was the Southern California Scientology Center on L. Ron Hubbard Drive. It took up two city blocks. A huge blinking sign read "Welcome. Your Future Is Up to You." I wondered about mine as I started toward the hospital. It all seemed surreal. Tuesday I was fine, and today I was getting hand surgery. My stomach growled from fasting.

At the surgery check-in, they took my clothes and wallet, put them in a plastic bag, and tied them to the end of my hospital bed. Dr. Tram came in and marked my hand with a big purple marker. It said E.T. in big letters. I don't know what it stood for, but I thought of the movie, and my hand was so ugly it seemed fitting. Later I found out they were his initials. I guess they do this so they don't operate on the wrong hand and know who to blame if they do.

When Dr Tram left, he drew the circular curtain around my bed, and I was alone in what felt like a holding cell. I thought of the chaplain work with the UCLA Care Committee. For three hours I lay in the gown I'd seen so many others wear. It gave me a new perspective on the isolation.

I was nervous and uneasy. I'd just dozed off when I heard the unmistakable laugh.

"Kusala," a voice said loudly from behind the curtain, and when the drape pulled back, there stood Deadra with a nurse.

"Deadra?" I said, half afraid. "What are you doing here?"

"Hey, Rev. Dang, they gotcha strapped in, huh?" she said, motioning to the IV.

"How did you know where I was?"

She wasn't the last person I'd want there, but definitely one of them.

"I saw Rebecca; she told me. You scared?" Deadra was wearing her platform heels and clomped over to the bed. The nurse left smiling with the totally wrong impression.

Deadra looked me over. I felt a bit odd in the hospital gown in front of her.

"I need a chair," she said and clomped back out into the hallway.

"Hey, okay if I use this?" she yelled to someone.

Inside voice, I thought. *Deadra, use your inside voice.*

She popped back in with a chair from the lobby and took a seat next to the bed.

"How did you find me?" I asked.

"I'm resourceful," she said.

Deadra dug into her purse and rummaged through like it was a closet. "I brought you this," she said, pulling out a granola bar. And Marcus sent this." It was an issue of *Tricycle: The Buddhist Review*.

I was shocked at her kindness. The granola bars were my favorite kind.

"I like these," I told her.

"I know. I see them in your trash all the time," she said.

"Perfect for when I can eat again," I said.

When the doctor came in, he stood over the bed and spoke to us like we were a couple. He gave us a quick rundown on how it would go and the time involved and ended with, "Will you be paying by check today?"

Deadra had to write out the $1,500 check because my hand was too swollen. I couldn't even hold a pen.

She stayed with me for two hours until they came in and wheeled me into pre-op.

She walked with me all the way to the operating doors, at which point the doctor said, "Okay, give him a kiss goodbye." When Deadra leaned down to give me a kiss, every bone in my body shrank a size.

"Just kiddin', Rev," she said and burst into a laugh.

Inside the operating room, I met the anesthesiologist. I'd thought the surgery required only a local anesthetic, but that's not what the anesthesiologist said.

"There's no way around it. A bacterial infection is tricky. Opening up the bite can stimulate it, so the only safe option is to have you under in case things look difficult once we're in." He walked toward me with a mask in his hand.

"I'm a little concerned about it altering my consciousness," I said.

He looked at me oddly.

"I meditate," I added. "Can't we just use local and whiskey?"

He smiled. "I'll give you just a little bit then," he said, and all I remember was that smile and counting backward.

When I awoke about two hours later, Deadra came back into post-op to say hello and brought my bag of clothes. I was groggy from the anesthesia. The doctor came over and said that there appeared to be only a small infected area, so all went well.

Deadra left around midnight, and I was grateful she'd been there. Doing that sort of thing alone is, well, I thought of Joe being alone in the V.A. ward before he died. The whole experience gave me insight into how important it is to be there for someone who is sick and afraid. The chaplain work now seemed more important than ever.

When I was cleared to go home, one of the sangha members came to give me a ride back to the center. She'd come armed with a bean burrito, and I was hungry. Again, I was overwhelmed by the small acts of kindness from the most unlikely of places.

For eight years, I was part of the Spiritual Care Committee at UCLA Medical Center, which meant giving talks to medical professionals and incoming chaplains about death and dying from a Buddhist perspective. In most cases, the only exposure the other chaplains had to Buddhism was fifteen minutes or so in the comparative religion classes they took in college. So my role on the Spiritual Care Committee was to give a short presentation about Buddhist priorities and practices concerning sickness and death. I rather liked giving these presentations. The Spiritual Care Department had asked me to be "big" and "animated," to fill the room rather than to sit on a cushion and just talk. It was hard to get used to at first, and sometimes I felt a bit "show businessy," but using humor when talking about death keeps people interested.

One day the talk went especially well. The best talks always managed to make Buddhism sound relevant and digestible. It was just one of those magical afternoons when everything came out effortlessly.

After the talk, there were accolades and smiles, and I found I was feeling rather satisfied with myself when one of the last remaining chaplains approached. She was a petite thin Christian woman with graying hair and spectacles who introduced herself as Michele.

"That was a wonderful talk," she said.

"Thank you," I said in a "meet the press" kind of way.

"I was wondering if you had some time to walk over to hospital, There's a twenty-four-year-old woman who's interested in Buddhism, and I'd love for her to meet you."

I looked at my watch; it was 3 p.m. on Friday, which meant if I stayed any longer, it would take two hours to get back to the center, rather than forty-five minutes.

"Today is busy," I said. "I could come back though."

"She's only got about two months," she said. "She's got advanced cancer." Her words teetered like a man on a wire.

"Oh," I said. "She's twenty-four?"

Michele nodded.

"Okay then, let's go," I said.

We walked across campus and spoke about the weather and buildings. When we approached the patient's room, Michele knocked quietly on the door, and a woman poked her head out.

"Hi," Michele said. "Is she up?"

The woman stepped out into the hallway and closed the door behind her.

"This is Kusala," Michele said.

The woman looked at me warmly and put her hands together, giving a slight bow hello. "I'm Julia," she said quietly.

Julia was kind-eyed and in her mid-forties.

"Not sure she's actually up. She was going in and out."

Julia had an uncommon strength about her, despite her uncombed hair and caregiver eye bags.

"And just a warning: she's a little angry sometimes," Julia said as she opened the door.

"Aria, this is Kusala."

I was still flying from my presentation, but when I saw Aria's face, that momentum fell away, grounding me with a thud. "Hi," I said, walking into the room.

Aria lay tethered to the bed by IVs and tubes. Twenty-four years old. Dead in two months. Her eyes traced my robes, and as we looked at each other, she saw what was going on inside me. I was digesting her sad reality.

The talk I'd given only moments before concerning the future of patient care was no use to a person without a future. For Aria, the final pencil stroke was happening, and she was just waiting for it to lift from the page. No wonder she was angry.

I stood there doing nothing and earned an iota of credit by avoiding further pleasantries. Her mother, Julia, excused herself for a coffee, and Aria and I were left alone. I walked to the door and set it ajar with the doorstop; after ordination, I was often uncomfortable when alone in a room with a woman. The open door eased my anxiety.

Aria was entangled in tubes and surrounded by tanks, and her room felt like some cryogenics lab created by Ridley Scott. She just lay there, staring at me.

I still couldn't find anything to say, so I just sat down and waited for something to happen. But nothing did.

Aria was blonde like her mother, and she'd been a teenage figure skater with a promising career as an Olympian until the tumor in her spine. They'd done surgery immediately, and there was a slight chance she'd never walk again; she never did. The cancer had metastasized, so not only had she been bedridden for eighteen months, she now had only two months left to live.

Our first day together lasted about fifteen minutes. When she asked what being a Buddhist really meant, I went into my usual monologue, which was more like the "history of Buddhism." Halfway through, I realized this was a huge mistake. She didn't have time or energy to digest any of these concepts; her eyes glazed over, and I was a bit ashamed of my lack of understanding of how rhetoric must sound to someone in her situation.

"Do you have any specific belief system you were raised with?" I asked.

She shook her head.

"Do you have any questions?"

Aria shrugged, and we took in a bit more of the quiet.

Eventually Julia came through the door stirring a Styrofoam cup of coffee. "The coffee is actually good; it's from that coffee cart," she said, dropping onto the cot in the corner. They'd set up a bed for her in Aria's room, and she had basically been living there.

"I thought Styrofoam was outlawed?" I said.

"Apparently not. Did you see that movie *An Inconvenient Truth*?" she asked.

We talked about the Guggenheim movie for a few moments, and it was a nice break.

Julia's energy was the perfect balance of sincerity and equanimity for the room. I admired how soft-spoken and concise she was, considering it was such a draining and heartfelt predicament.

When I stood to leave, I looked back at Aria and realized she'd never lifted her head from the pillow.

"I'll be back over for a meeting on Tuesday," I said. "If you'd like me to stop in, I could?"

Julia looked at Aria for approval. "That'd be great," Julia translated.

I took about fourteen steps down the hallway before one of the nurses saw me.

"You okay?" she asked.

"That was a hard one," I said.

She shook her head. "I know, it doesn't seem fair."

"I've cried more in the last eight years than I have in my whole life because of this chaplain stuff," I said.

She touched my shoulder the way only nurses can. "That's why we need you here. Volunteers are opting in from the heart. You can be with the patients differently. As staff, lots of us compartmentalize our emotions into the box of 'professionalism' That's how I cope. The chaplains, though, you don't have that luxury. You're showing up for people who are in the saddest of circumstances. You all volunteer to just stand there with them."

This was helpful to hear, because often I felt like I had failed somehow if emotions crept out of me when I was around the sick or dying.

After the Tuesday chaplain meeting, I went across the way to Aria's room to find the door ajar. I looked in to see if she was up and saw two nurses dressing a bedsore on the back of Aria's arm.

I closed the door quietly and waited in the hall. Twenty-four-year-olds are supposed to be finding an internship, breaking up with boyfriends, getting their first new couch, not fighting off the searing pain of bedsores. When the two nurses came out, they told me she'd gone to sleep, which seemed unbelievable. I soon realized that was code for "she needed a sedative," which was often the only way to relieve such pain.

"Is it okay if I leave this in there for her mom?" I asked.

The nurses looked at the small Buddha statue

"She asked me to bring it," I said, feeling like some pushy missionary. "Or could you just leave it in there for me?"

"Go on in," the nurse said.

I took about three steps into the room and put the statue onto the counter.

As I began to head to the parking lot, Julia rounded the corner in the hallway.

"Are you leaving?" she asked.

"Arias asleep."

"She's looking forward to your visit," she said.

"I was looking forward to it as well."

"Whatever you two talked about really shifted her mood. She's been asking all week if it's Tuesday."

This was a surprise since Aria and I had mostly been silent with each other. "How are you doing?" I asked.

"I don't know," she said, tugging at one of her sleeves.

"Do you have family helping you?" I asked.

"You're help," she said. "Her father lives in Texas. He's a birthday card kind of dad. He came early on after the first surgery, but I don't know if he'll come again."

Julia looked at her phone.

"I'm waiting for a work call. They're letting me know if we get to keep our insurance. They say I've been on leave too long."

She exhaled, tired. "I cry too much if I stop moving." She pushed open Aria's door and walked in.

Aria was lying there asleep.

"She may be out for a while," I said.

"I'm not deaf," Aria said without opening her eyes.

"Ohhh, an eavesdropper," I said lightly.

"It's not eavesdropping when you can see I'm right here, Bhikshu."

She groggily opened her eyes.

Julia brought over a cup of water for Aria. "Use the straw," she said.

"Shut up," Aria cracked.

Julia paused, got up, and left the room with the door hanging open. Aria drank the water cup dry.

"Want more?" I asked.

"No," she said.

"You want to be alone?"

"I already am," she said.

"Is that how it feels?"

"Yep, and don't give me any of that feel-good shit, thank you very much."

"I don't know what feel-good talk I could give to you, Aria," I said, feeling strange.

And then, ever so softly, Aria said "fuck you" under her breath.

"Are you sure that was just water?" I said, standing up, collecting my things.

She shot me a glance of some twenty-four-year-old attitude.

"What do you think happens on the other side?" she blurted.

"I don't think of it as another side. I think death might be more of a process than an event or place. I like to think of it like there's no longer heads or tails. It's just the whole coin at that point. Maybe more of an interconnected thing?"

She looked annoyed at the answer.

"You know what's hard?" she said. "Knowing this is

the last room I'll ever be in. This is it. There's nothing but here, nobody but you, fucking doctors, my fucking mom. I'll never walk across the grass outside again."

Her words pinged my heart; the truth can ring the harshest of bells.

"You want to go outside?" I asked.

"No! I want to walk to a train track, have you dump me out like a wheelbarrow, and leave me there."

"I can't imagine this is anything less than torture."

"Yeah, and why can't something save me? All you religious people talk about love and some all-loving god, but this happens every goddamn day to someone. Your god, or Buddha, has a pretty sick sense of humor."

My head dropped, and I looked at my shoes. I thought of what the nurse had said; I was a volunteer.

"Do you want to be alone?" I asked again.

"No, I want you to stay here and answer me," she said.

It was hard to be around someone so angry.

"I thought you were supposed to relieve suffering?" she said.

I didn't know what to say.

"Aren't you?" she prodded.

"What do you think suffering is?" I asked her.

"I don't know; you tell me."

"It's when you want things different than they are."

She was listening.

"In every situation," I continued, "there is a chance for peace."

"Happiness?"

"No, not happiness, just peace. It's acceptance, even in this unfair world."

"And how do I find that here in this bed, just before I die?"

"Sometimes, inside, you might see the possibility of a place that's uniquely yours and peaceful. A refuge."

"Why does God let this happen?"

"I once asked a priest the same thing, a question about freedom of choice, and he said God gives us choice in how to respond to circumstances; we're not puppets on a string. It's not predestined. It's a choice of how we respond."

"I don't have a choice about how I feel. How am I supposed to get my choice back?"

"Meditation can give us our choice back sometimes. We sit quietly, allowing the good and bad stuff to arise in our mind, exist, and pass away. At the end, all we see is stuff; we stop owning."

"I've no use for stuff now," she said.

"It's about your mind stuff. It creates stories, and stories create us."

"I just want to live," she said dryly.

"What is life?"

She looked at me blankly. "What do you think it is?"

"According to Buddhism, life consists of impermanence, not self, and suffering. It's always changing, always in a state of flux, and all the people we've ever been are different moment to moment. It's a big circle, no beginning, no end."

"You're seriously exhausting," she said, clenching her jaw. It had been a long day, and I was happy to be heading back to the center. When I arrived, there were two things waiting for me: large box of expensive cat food that had been donated from a podcast listener, and Deryl. He was there to talk.

"Hi ya, Deryl," I said, trodding up the steps. "How's it going?"

"I've become enlightened, Kusala," he said.

I stopped short, waiting for him to say he was just kidding.

"Really?" was all I mustered.

Deryl had been coming to the center for a few years. He was a regular at meditation and Sunday services, but I hadn't seen him around since the winter. He had never seemed like a whack job; in fact he rarely said much.

"Yeah, I was meditating and there was this…. there was this thing that came over me. And now everything is way different."

"When did it happen?" I asked, trying not to sound antagonizing.

"I think about two months ago. That's why I haven't been here. I'm so in the present moment, it's hard to drive," he said.

The smell of pickle juice wafted up from the groceries I was carrying. A wet stain had started to bleed through the paper bag. I put the sack down and started to investigate.

Deryl continued. "I've had to quit my job too. I'm on unemployment though, and I'm the happiest I've ever been."

"How's Jen liking the new you?" I asked.

"We've moved in together, and she's working full time, so it's perfect."

"But you're not working?" I said, repacking the groceries.

"I can't work, Kusala. You…" He searched for words. "…You can't understand."

Given I am a monastic, I felt obliged to ask about his claim.

"I'm not here to tell you that you're not enlightened, Deryl, but if enlightenment meant you couldn't function in the world, who would want it?"

"It's okay. I can't put it into words." He smiled with a bit of smugness.

"Why do you think being unable to work is a sign of enlightenment?" I asked. I didn't have much in the way of patience. Hospice does that to me.

He shrugged. "It just is."

I felt a twinge of anger. "No job, can't drive, unable to function on a critical level. Is that what you spent all that time trying achieve when you were coming here? The Buddha worked harder after his Nirvana, not less."

"Hey, peace to you, brother," he said.

"I'd really think about what you're saying, before you go saying it all over the place."

Deryl walked off ,and I noticed he was wearing a hip new pair of Reeboks.

"New shoes?" I asked.

He nodded. I shook my head.

The following Monday, I got a call from Julia to see if I'd be coming.

"I wasn't sure she wanted me there last time," I said.

"She does. She keeps asking when you're coming by."

In the background, I heard Aria say, "Tell him I do."

It was a light week, so I arrived the following day.

"So is this happening because my karma's bad?" Aria asked.

"No, it doesn't work like that. There are ten thousand reasons why any one thing happens. In Buddhism, there's never a single cause."

"So if my karma was good, it wouldn't matter then?"

"Well, karma is complex. The sutras say there are about five things that the human mind will go insane trying to think about. One of them is trying to understand karma. It operates non-linearly, and while it's a law, like gravity, it's somewhat indirect, and accounts for past life experiences. Only a Buddha who is fully awakened is said to understand karma."

"Do you ever say anything that's straightforward?"

"No." I smiled.

"Very funny. So if karma is only one of the reasons, why is everyone always talking about it?"

"Well, it's not unimportant, it's just not the only cause for things. Karma is everything that we think, say, and do, so it's something we have the most control over. Other things, not so much. "

Julia came in blowing her nose and lay down on her cot.

"Mom, Kusala says I might have cancer because of your bad karma. I'm paying for it."

Stiffness sang through the room.

"I'm just kidding!" Aria jabbed.

Julia threw a pillow in Aria's face. "You're drugged and an easy target," she laughed.

"Yeah, Aria," I said. "You can't even walk. Maybe you shouldn't crack on people who can." For those few moments the cancer had left the room.

We said our goodbyes, and Aria's eyes looked brighter than I'd seen them.

Although I left there feeling happier than when I arrived, I also had a gnawing feeling that things were about to change. After all, they always do.

Aria held on much longer than two months; it was going on four. Julia was exhausted. She was forced to return to work in order to keep their insurance. She was a court stenographer, and when she dressed in her skirt suit, it was clearly only a gesture to accommodate protocols. She'd lost so much weight from the stress that the suit hung off her frame like a scarecrow.

When I arrived the following week, there was a handwritten sign on Aria's door that said "no visitors." The nurse said that Aria had developed some scabbing on the back of her head, and they were forced to shave off her hair. She was mortified and didn't want anyone to see her.

I came back a few days later to find an older-looking, sicker Aria, and without her hair, the illness was right there; her thin skin had settled like silt around her facial bones.

"You trying to be a nun at the last minute?" I asked, rubbing my bald head.

"Hi," she said quietly.

"Hi," I said back.

"Not a good look," she said.

She smiled weakly and then went into a coughing spasm. It was a hard visit, and we didn't have much to say. She was in and out, and I left with a pit in my stomach. Aria was dying more quickly now.

That night, her lung collapsed from fluid, and she went into surgery. I came the next day. She talked to me with her eyes closed.

"I just want it over."

"It'll be over soon," I said.

"I don't wanna come back," she said.

"Neither do I," I said.

"What do you think I'll come back as?"

"My guess? A turtle. You were sort of a trouble maker, I think, so this way you'll be slow, unlikely to cause anyone any problems," I said.

"I like turtles," she whispered, opening her eyes and looking out the window as if she were saying goodbye to some unseen thing.

"I'm sorry I was rude to you."

"It's okay. One of the things you called me I'd never even heard before, so no harm there," I said.

"Why do what you do, Kusala?"

I was quiet, trying not to cry.

"It doesn't matter," she said.

"It does matter," I stammered. "I'm glad we got a chance to meet."

She nodded.

For the last week, Aria was pretty out of it. The cancer was now in her liver, hip, throat, and lung. She was asleep most of the time and would occasionally thrash violently, like Princess did in the cardboard box before she passed.

Most days I just sat there so Julia wasn't alone. I hardly found words to offer, but Julia always thanked me for coming and asked when I'd return.

The night before Aria passed was an IBMC open meditation night, and while meditating, a peace fell over me like a shadow. The next morning Julia called to tell me that Aria was gone.

As I fed the cats that morning, I felt relieved for everyone, but a strange, slow, undertone hummed from somewhere inside me. I think it was the news, but also I was just plain tired. I'd forgotten that the man from NPR was coming to pick up my motorcycle, and when he arrived, it was a welcome shift in the day.

I'd been thinking of donating the bike for a while. A friend of mine had been hit while riding and now had irreversible brain damage. I was older now, and it seemed like a good time to let the bike go. I'd made arrangements to donate it to NPR a month earlier but had forgotten to write it down.

As I watched the bike get strapped to the flatbed truck, I felt a pang of resistance. I'd had a motorcycle for over twenty years, and my ego wasn't ready to let that side of me go. "This means you're really old now," it said, "boring, average." An unexpected sadness perched inside me as I watched the bike disappear down the street and around the corner.

I walked back through the zendo past the Buddha and was reminded how strong self-grasping can be. It was late morning now, and with Aria gone, the bike gone, the cats fed, it felt like a good time to rest.

As I came out the back porch door into the yard, I paused, taking in the scene. Carl was off on the far side in the grass, quietly dancing between Dr Pepper cans. Deadra sat reading a magazine at her patio table. Rain was curled up under the steps of the bell tower, and Marcus sat in the farthest corner by the koi pond.

I felt a simple and profound harmony that played against the drum of loss, all of us in the backyard, in the same pale shine of the March sun, separate but together somehow. The moment was whole and graceful, the sadness of life having rolled into a larger painting.

As I made my way to a lawn chair, I noticed a seedling had pushed up through the dead leaves of winter, and as I took a seat in the middle of the lawn, I felt part of eternity in a way that was truly easy.

Deadra was the first to peel off; she left through the side gate. Carl went inside soon after. Marcus and I still shared the yard until he stood, stretched his arms overhead, and started toward the Quan Yin House.

"You okay?" he said, pausing as he passed my chair.

"I am," I said.

He looked at me like he wanted me to say something more.

"What's your story, Marcus?" I asked. "What are you doing here?"

He shifted his stance and looked away. I could see his wheels turning.

"I don't know," he said, searching for words.

He looked toward the back fence and again shifted on his feet. "For the last few years, I've been part of a lot of film projects that were, well, successful," he said humbly.

We all knew what he'd done and that he had made a decent amount of money.

"But not in all ways," he continued. "I mean, they've made money but I . . . they feel meaningless."

I nodded in understanding.

"Isn't there a way to pick and choose what you're involved in?"

"Well, that's sort of what I'm doing here," he said. "I'm doing research."

"Oh, you doing your next movie on Buddhism?" I asked.

"Well, that's part of it," he said. "Actually I'm researching you."

I felt I'd fallen asleep and woken up in mid-conversation.

"Me?" I said, confused.

"You ever think about doing a book, Kusala?"

"No, not really." I said

Further Reading

I've included a list below of further reading, including *The Grand Ordination of 1994*, by Ven. Dr. Karuna Dharma, which chronicles the day I was ordained and the immense effort that went into IBMC's first formal round of monastic ordinations. You'll also find a history of IBMC's College of Buddhist Studies, the formal degree-conferring school I attended that operated from IBMC for twenty years. Next is a brief biography of IBMC's founder, Venerable Thich Thien-An, and the *Los Angeles Times* obituary of my main teacher, Venerable Dr. Ratanasara. Lastly, I've highlighted Ven. Sarika Dharma, who was instrumental in giving women and, most notably, lesbian women a role model and place in American Buddhism.

1. *The Grand Ordination of 1994*, by Ven. Dr. Karuna Dharma.

2. A history of IBMC's College of Buddhist Studies, 1982-2002: http://www.urbandharma.org/ibmc/ibmc1/cbs.html

3. A biography of IBMC's founder, Venerable Thich Thien-An: https://urbandharma.org/pdf11/Thien-An.pdf

4. An obituary of Kusala's main teacher ("U.S. Buddhism Leader Havanpola Ratanasara Dies," by Elaine Woo, *The Los Angeles Times*): https://www.latimes.com/archives/la-xpm-2000-jun-02-me-36637-story.html

5. A biography of Ven. Sarika Dharma, an American nun who led the way for lesbians in Buddhism: http://www.urbandharma.org/ibmc/ibmc1/nunk.html

Acknowledgments

"We shall not cease from exploration, and the end of all our exploring will be to arrive where we started and know the place for the first time." —*T. S. Eliot*

G ratitude is the recognition of the interconnectedness and interdependence of all phenomena. It's about understanding that you are never on this journey alone. There will be people along the way who will help you whether you recognize their help or not. It also means that you can't take full credit for anything since we do nothing alone.

The first person I'm grateful to is Huston Smith, author of *The World's Religions,* where I first read about Buddhism. I read the whole chapter in one sitting.

Many years later, I had a chance to meet Huston when he was making a presentation at UCLA and told him that his book changed the course of my life. I remain forever grateful to him for writing the book.

The second person who dramatically shaped my religious life was my first teacher, Shinzen Young, who holds a Ph.D.

in Buddhist Studies from the University of Wisconsin and lived for three years in a Japanese monastery on Mount Koya as an ordained Shingon (Japanese Vajrayana) monk while doing his thesis. Shinzen gave the first dharma talk I had ever heard, and because English was his first language, he was easy for me to understand. He planted the idea that life could be experienced in a magical way, that our culture or our families do not predetermine it, but that we have the option to change ourselves through our Buddhist practice.

The third person I'm grateful to is my main dharma teacher, Dr. Ratanasara, a Theravada elder from Sri Lanka who lived at a monastery from the age of thirteen. In 1957, he became the first monk at the United Nations when Sri Lanka designated him as the country's representative. Dr. Ratanasara was a true scholar who held a Ph.D; after coming stateside in 1980, he founded the College of Buddhist Studies. I met him in 1983 and worked to learn Buddhism from him for almost twenty years, until he passed in 2000. Under his guidance, I eventually got my Bachelor of Arts in Buddhist Studies, and it was he who suggested that I take ordination. He taught me about being a monastic by what he did, not by what he said. He showed me that vows procure freedom rather than suffering and helped me find a life that was of benefit to myself and, most importantly, others. My gratitude for his help is inexpressible.

The fourth person I'm grateful to is Jeff Gold, the record executive who loaned me the money to buy my first computer in 1988. Without his kind offer, I likely would not have the web presence I have today. My website has over two thousand pages, my podcasts average about fifteen thousand downloads a month, and my Facebook page has thirty thousand followers as of August 2023. Jeff affected thousands of lives over the years with his generosity, and I continue to marvel at what one gesture of kindness can set in motion.

The fifth person I'd like to thank is the late Venerable Karuna Dharma, a student of Ven. Dr. Thich Thien-An and one of the first American women to take full ordination in the Vietnamese Zen tradition. Rev. Karuna Dharma became the abbess of IBMC in 1980 when Venerable Thien-An passed, and she ran the center for over thirty years.

Looking back, I didn't appreciate her nearly enough. I considered Shinzen and Dr. Ratanasara to be my main dharma teachers, and even though Rev. Karuna Dharma was a teacher too, I viewed her mainly as my boss while I worked as a residential manager and monk at IBMC. But the reality is, she was possibly the most important supporter of my dharma practice. There is no way I would have had the time or means to lead the life of a monk without her kind offer of a salary, health insurance, and lodging. Venerable Karuna Dharma gave me a place to fail, a place to succeed, and a small enough pond to be a big fish in.

I'm immensely grateful to all the people who send me donations, who give money toward supporting the cats, and who have asked me to speak over the last few decades. I'm also grateful to my parents and my family, and most certainly to the Buddha dharma.

As we part ways on the page, I send you off with these wishes:

May suffering ones be suffering free, and
the fear struck fearless be.
May the grieving shed all grief, and the sick find health relief.

Rebecca Wilson wishes to thank the following people for shaping her life path:

His Holiness the Dalai Lama, Khyongla Rato, Khensur Rinpoche Lobzang Tsetan, Nicholas Vreeland, Kusala Bhikshu, Robert Thruman, Tony Spina, Ken Small, William A. Wilson, Kayla Samascott-Wilson, Betty & Horace Ransom, my mom Patricia Wilson, Barbara Resch, Cowgirl Morgan Rumler-Wilson, Sara Crisp, Karen Macrae, Ed Pastorini, Ken Freeman, mama bear Bette Austin, Ms. Sparky Mary Stapleton, Maggie Hill, Michele Atkins & Joe Paganelli, Carol Ransom, Bill Wilson, Joy Vaughan, Kate Lutzner, Alex & Sarah Nahas, Dean Russell, Janita Maria, Yoav Ben Yosef, Laura Kozaitis, Jeff Zaxs, William Fitzpatrick & family, Pascal Pelat, Kristen Roupenian, Debbie Peterson, Judith Ransom, Jon Bendis, Matt Gerald, Victor Salvo, Corey Hajim & Jim Sperber, Stephen Scaringe & Sarah Morelli, Andrew Wilson, Hunter & Brooke Wilson, the tattoo king Russel Hayden, Sydney Young, Alex Stigliano, Jody/Ron/Jake/Laurie Samascott, Vicki Peterson, Lissa Coffey, Heidi Doorman, Cheryl Kanekar, Chris Sprague, Snehy Gupta, Jayda Novak, Neil Kendricks, IBMC Doug, Christine Lafuente, Barbra Allen, Michael Nigro, John Cowsill, Laurie House, Marie Bresnahan, Steve Varney, Missy & Justin, Lauren & George, and finally, Ron, the guy in the security booth at Greenwood Cemetery who always had a smile when I arrived for my afternoon walk.

Printed in Poland
by Amazon Fulfillment
Poland Sp. z o.o., Wrocław